The Time of Your Life

The Time of Your Life

Self / Time Management for Pastors

LINCOLN CHRISTIAN COLLEGE AND SEMINARY

ROBERT L. RANDALL

Abingdon Press
Nashville

THE TIME OF YOUR LIFE
SELF/TIME MANAGEMENT FOR PASTORS

Copyright © 1994 by Abingdon Press

This book is printed on acid-free, recycled paper.

Library of Congress Cataloging-in-Publication Data

Randall, Robert L., 1942-
    The time of your life : self/time management for pastors / Robert L. Randall.
        p.   cm.
    Includes bibliographical references.
    ISBN 0-687-37137-6 (pbk. : alk. paper)
    1. Clergy—Time management.   I. Title.
    BV4379.5.R36   1994
    253'.2—dc20   93-45856
                                                                              CIP

94 95 96 97 98 99 00 01 02 03 — 10 9 8 7 6 5 4 3 2 1

MANUFACTURED IN THE UNITED STATES OF AMERICA

My deep appreciation to Norman Shawchuck for taking time from his own writing projects to offer the foreword to this book. Many of us know Norman by reputation. It is my good fortune to begin to know him as a colleague.

My thanks also to a longtime partner in ministry, Richard Wolf, for his editorial help. It's a joy to be able now to call him "Dr. Wolf."

Contents

FOREWORD. 9
INTRODUCTION: Life Time 11

CHAPTER ONE: Self-Management:
Maintaining Self-Cohesion. 17

Self-Cohesion and Time. 18
Levels of Self-Cohesion 21
Fluctuations in Self-Cohesion. 23
Being Wise and Affirming 24

CHAPTER TWO: Time Management:
Dimensions in Ministry 28

Levels of Time Management. 29
    Owning Time. 30
    Rendering Time 32
    Using Time. 34
    Creating Time 35
    Sensing Time. 37
    Revealing Time 39
Assessing Self/Time Management. 41
Ultimate Purpose of Time Management 43

CHAPTER THREE: Self/Time Management
in Pastoral Care. 47

Self-Cohesion and Pastoral Care. 48
Being Wise About Ourself. 50
    Monitoring Guilt. 50
    Monitoring Criticisms 52
    Monitoring Needs for Specialness 54
Being Wise About Others. 56
    Managing Emergencies 56
    Managing Selfobject Expectations 58
Affirming Ourself 63

Affirming One's Doing 64
Establishing Self-Affirmations 65
Affirming Others 66
Affirming Subjective Truth 67
Validating Intentions 68

CHAPTER FOUR: Self/Time Management
in Preaching 71
Self-Cohesion and Preaching 72
Being Wise About Ourself 75
Facing Creative Tensions 75
Employing Imagination 79
Being Wise About Others 82
Acknowledging Resistances to Change 83
Embracing Inspirational Decline 85
Affirming Ourself 90
Affirming Others 93

CHAPTER FIVE: Self/Time Management
in Church Administration 96
Self-Cohesion and Church Administration 97
Being Wise About Ourself 101
Monitoring Our Timing 102
Avoiding Executivism 104
Being Wise About Others 110
Affirming Ourself 115
Affirming Others 118

CHAPTER SIX: Self/Time Management
in Personal Maintenance 122
Self-Cohesion and Personal Maintenance 122
Being Wise About Ourself 124
Being Wise About Others 131
Affirming Ourself and Others 136

NOTES 139

SELECTED BIBLIOGRAPHY 141

Foreword

A person of great wisdom was asked by a young leader, "What is the greatest gift in the world?" Without hesitation the wise one replied, "To have all the time you need. But such a measure of time can be given to no one. Each person must help himself or herself to a portion and learn to use it wisely, else many of the blessings of this most precious of all gifts will be denied."

Time carries with it no guarantee that it will serve us. It is only made available for us to wisely manage. And manage it we must, or someone else surely will.

Dr. Randall brings a much needed perspective to this whole issue of time management. On the one hand, he reaffirms what we commonly know, namely that wise use of time in ministry is a stewardship matter. The blessings of the church's most precious gifts are lost when time is not effectively used. On the other hand, Randall lifts up what we need to know, namely that effective use of time is primarily determined by the state of the pastor's self. Time management skills or techniques only go so far. The pastor's interior life is the crucial factor shaping how time is approached in ministry. Adequate time management requires self-management. This book is about that greatest and hardest preparation of all—the preparation within.

Another important theme rumbles in this book, one that is quieter but still a heartbeat throughout. Self/time management is not only a stewardship act, not only a self-healing activity, but also a spiritual response. Randall never forgets that "the time of your life" is always set in

God's time. Self/time management is ultimately a response to God's call to live time fully and to live as a full self.

This book will be of invaluable help to pastors at any stage of their ministry. It assists all of us to become responsible for what happens inside us, and thus for what happens outside of us in our work. There is no alternative to this interior journey. It is reassuring to have Randall's companionship and guidance on this road of self/time management.

Norman Shawchuck
Leith, North Dakota

Introduction

Life Time

> For every matter has its time and way, although the troubles of mortals lie heavy upon them.
>
> ECCLESIASTES 8:6

The essence of time management is self-management. For pastors to manage time well, they must have effective control of their individual self. It is the state of a pastor's self that determines the pastor's responsiveness to time management issues in ministry.

Mass-market books on time management work from the outside in. They claim that improved external management of time will result in an improved inner life. Time management itself, however, should not be confused with life enhancement. A pastor's improved control of time may bring about a better coordinated sequence of activities, but that does not ensure the essential thing, namely living fully, and helping parishioners live fully, the time of our lives.

This book, in contrast, works from the inside out. It attempts to help us clergy enhance our inner life so that we can become better stewards of time in our ministry. When we become more cohesive and understanding selves, we can respond more empathically to the time-related needs of parishioners, and to our own time needs.

These pages, therefore, are dedicated to ordained ministers who sense that a resourceful use of time is a personal issue. Their honest appraisal confirms that internal time stealers (fear of criticism, resistance to change, or tendencies toward perfectionism, for example) are more the culprits than external time stealers (unexpected calls, too many meetings, or inadequate church staff). This book joins with pastors' desires to enhance their self-management and thus improve their personal and professional approaches to time.

To accomplish this, we look at key dimensions of the pastor's ministry: pastoral care, preaching, church administration, and personal maintenance. In each situation we consider how the minister can be "wise and affirming." On the one hand, pastors maintain their self-cohesion by being wise, that is, being guided by mature insights about themselves and parishioners in each area of pastoral work. On the other hand, pastors maintain their self-cohesion by being affirming, that is, genuinely appreciating themselves and parishioners in each act of ministry. When pastors respond with wisdom and affirmation, self-cohesion is preserved. When self-cohesion is preserved, time-related matters are handled adequately. Time management is self-management.

Time management in this book means more than the ordained minister's effort to reduce work time and increase efficiency. It involves a broader, pastorally relevant sense of time management. It means, for example, responding effectively to the time-related events of parishioners, guiding persons in the psychological and spiritual significance of their time, helping the church be a good steward of its communal time in worship, service, and administration, and practicing healthy time commitments in the pastor's own personal life. Time management is ministering effectively to the self-time needs of parishioners and pastor.

Unfortunately time management in the church is often problematic. First, a pastor's inadequate time usage disturbs parishioners. Congregations expect proficiency from their pastor, along with the ability to prioritize tasks. Time is a measuring rod parishioners use to judge the competence and achievements of the pastor. While this might seem unfair to clergy, difficulties in managing time and delays in reaching goals are interpreted as professional/personal weaknesses. Tolerance for these weaknesses stretches only so far.

For parishioners, time is also a special message system revealing how the pastor feels about them. A brief visit by the pastor may suggest to a parishioner a lack of interest, for example. Long sermons may be taken as signs of the preacher's ego rather than of the preacher's concern for the congregation. A pastor's sensitivity to the time-linked events of parishioners, however, is deeply appreciated, such as remembering the time of year and date of a loved one's death. How the minister lives time with parishioners shapes the relationship with them, for good or ill.

Furthermore, parishioners experience their time as a possession. Like the ownership of their bodies, they feel an ownership of their hours and days. When their time is violated, they feel personally violated. Forms of depletion and rage arise when their precious life-time is taken from them by the pastor.

Parishioners also experience themselves as temporal beings, as unfolding selves made up of past, present, and future. When a parishioner loses the continuity of his or her life, such as through a stroke that eradicates part of memory, or through a sudden life change that challenges self-identity, that parishioner loses a sense of self to some degree. Confusion and panic set in whenever feelings of sameness through time are disturbed.

Parishioners expect ordained ministers to be sensitive to these self-time needs. Anything pastors do that affirms temporal continuity strengthens pastor-parish relationships. Conversely, anything pastors do that disrupts persons' temporal continuity erodes trust in the pastor.

Second, time management can become a problem when the pastor's self-esteem is threatened. Many clergy berate themselves for being disorganized. Not only may they feel deficient, they may also feel unfaithful. Love of God should result in dutiful service, they avow. A beseeching line from an old hymn may stand as condemnation: "And let our ordered lives confess the beauty of thy peace."

As a result, clergy may frantically strive to be "efficient." Their goal becomes one of trying to get more things done in a shorter length of time. Unfortunately this time management effort not only tends to fail in the long run, thus contributing to more self-incriminations, but it also detracts from what should have been the primary goal in the first place, namely "effectiveness." Faithful pastors strive to get the *right* things done, not necessarily the *most* things done. They strive to respond at the *right* time, not necessarily in the *quickest* time. Pastors struggle in their work when their self-esteem is low and time management efforts are misdirected.

Third, time management can become a problem when "time" is a misguided diagnosis. Pastors and parishioners frequently try to manage conflict (and the anxiety that such conflict generates) by diagnosing the problem as one of time. The congregation may complain about the pastor's lack of time at the church. The pastor may complain that the church wants too much time. Time itself, however, is often not the direct problem. It is what time means to the self of the congregation and to the self of the pastor that is crucial. Time may really mean the parish's need for the pastor's consistently available soothing presence. Time for the pastor may mean the freedom to move from place to place outside the church for needed doses of affirmation.[1] A suggestion that the pastor take a time management course as a means for healing the conflict not only fails to address the heart of the matter, but may also increase the frustration of all concerned. Once again, time management issues always refer to the condition of someone's self.

Finally, time management becomes a problem when it represents the primacy of functionalism in the church. Functionalism dominates in a church when the primary effort is to enhance the functioning of the church's programs and policies. A corporate mentality that focuses on efficient church structure and implementation can supplant a ministry dedicated to meeting the needs of people.[2]

Time management strategies can be symptomatic of a pastor or congregation having moved away from a ministry by faithfulness to a ministry by objective. Establishing yearly goals becomes more important than an effort to serve faithfully. Allotment of time becomes more important than meaningful involvement. The management of people becomes more important than caring for persons. We must be alert to the character of time management techniques in the church. They may create problems rather than resolve them.

Our effort to enhance the pastor's self/time management begins with chapter 1 outlining the essence of self-management—namely maintaining self-cohesion. Chapter 2 highlights the essential dimensions of time management in ministry. Chapter 3 details self/time management in pastoral care, while chapters 4, 5, and 6 do the same for preaching, church administration, and personal maintenance, respectively.

The words of Ecclesiastes remind us clergy that the troubles of our selves can lie heavy upon the time of our lives. With God's help, our selves can be strengthened, allowing our pastoral matters to have their right time and way.

Chapter One

Self-Management
Maintaining Self-Cohesion

Reverend James was sermonless. Time had gotten away from him, and now he sat at his desk late Friday afternoon worried that he would not make it. Saturday could not save him. Family plans and an evening potluck at church demanded his attention. He had once looked forward to these events, but today they felt like burdens.

Trying to write Saturday night always left him drained on Sunday morning, and also a bit ashamed. He did not want to be seen, or to think of himself, as disorganized, or worse, incompetent. He shifted uneasily, remembering with embarrassment those times in seminary when he failed to make deadlines or turned in half-finished projects.

His mind was vacant as he read the biblical passage and skimmed the commentaries. No thoughts came to him; no sudden creative idea about what to say, how to be helpful, or how to preserve his reputation as a good preacher.

His stomach began to tighten. His heart picked up its pace, the way it always did when he felt somewhere on the edge of panic. He could feel his temperature rise and the wetness begin beneath his arms. The more anxious he became the more difficult it was to concentrate. His mind drifted off to an earlier meeting with a parishioner unhappy with worship. He stewed awhile about what trouble it might bring.

Trying to regroup, he energetically rearranged the papers on his desk, then stood up and walked briskly around his office, taking deep breaths. Sitting back down, he decided to make a few phone calls before beginning.

• • • • • • • • • •

Reverend Marten's hand was steady as she reached over to console the sobbing husband and two small children. The words of comfort she spoke felt genuine. The suggestions she made felt right. Without second thoughts, she stood up to go when she knew she had stayed long enough. While her heart ached for this motherless family, her faith in God's goodness seemed ever more strong. An assuredness about her calling and the worth of her ministry swept over her. She thought of how proud her old home pastor would have been to see his little confirmand now. With a mild shiver of delight she felt God's voice saying, "Well done, thou good and faithful servant." And she was thankful.

SELF-COHESION AND TIME

All of us in ministry can identify with these two self-states. Like Reverend James, we know what it's like when our sense of security is shaken. Events small to critical can disturb our equilibrium, leaving us uneasy, frazzled, or feeling that we're losing our grip.

In that condition, assured feelings about ourself begin to weaken. We start to doubt ourself, to wonder if we are as capable as we thought we were, or as special as we have envisioned ourself to be. Confidence in our understanding wanes. We become less certain that we can hold up physically to pressures. Our goals and ambitions, once a source of pride, lose something of their importance.

When our cohesion is disrupted, our feelings about others also darken. We start to think that others would be disappointed in us, if not reject us, if they really knew us. We begin to doubt whether anyone really understands, really cares for us, in the way they profess. Confidence in the goodness of others dwindles. Our relationships and loves, once a source of great comfort, lose something of their power. Like Reverend James, we become painfully aware of our moments of fragmentation.

Like Reverend Marten, we also know the experiences of self-assurance. At times we feel put together, confident, and strong. Difficult encounters touch us but do not adversely affect our firm sense of stability.

In that condition, we feel good about ourself. Our words and actions feel appropriate. We lean securely on our abilities and insights. We are comfortable with who we are. We zestfully embrace our work, loved ones, and goals. When faced with criticisms, we are able to maintain our equilibrium.

When our self-cohesion is firm, we also respond positively to others. We look for the good in them. We assume that they are doing the best they can. We identify with their struggles, and feel empathy for what they are going through. When they hurt us in some way, we are able to tolerate it and work for reconciliation.

The condition of ourself shapes not only how we feel about ourself or others, it also shapes how we use our time. When the cohesion of ourself is weakened, then our capacity to structure time and respond with sensitivity to time-related issues of parishioners is weakened. When the cohesion of ourself is strengthened, then our capacity to manage time adequately is strengthened. Understanding the pivotal role of self-cohesion and how it affects the use of time in ministry is critical for pastors. The clergy's ups and downs are not mysterious, but have meaning. More importantly, grasping that meaning is the first step toward restoration of pastors, and toward restoration of their parishioners as well.

The threat of not finishing his sermon adequately, or not finishing it at all, disturbed the cohesion of the Reverend James's self, and with it his effective use of time. He could not start. His mind drifted from the task. He ruminated about the future and the past rather than remaining in the present. His efforts to soothe himself led to further avoidance. The quality of his time with family and church was potentially jeopardized due to his disturbed self-state.

What Reverend James needed at that moment were not techniques for increasing his efficiency. He needed something to restore his self-cohesion. He was not suffering from the lack of time management skills; he was suffering from fragmentation of his self. His time problem was a self problem.

In contrast, Reverend Marten's firm self-cohesion made words and acts time-graced. Her attentive self knew how long to touch, how frequently to talk. She shaped the length of her stay and the rate of her speech to meet the temporal needs of the family. She made suggestions appropriate for the time of grief they were in. With thankfulness she recognized this moment as a divine moment, and opened herself to the power of God working through it.

What Reverend Marten needed at that moment was to

preserve the healthy cohesion of her self, which allowed all things to be done in good time. Well-managed time was a product of an intact self. Time management techniques could help her consolidate her self-cohesion, but they could not be a substitute for her firm self-cohesion.

Other capacities are enhanced or restored when the cohesion of a pastor's self is made firm: tolerance, awareness, playfulness, creativity, intimacy, and openness to the transcendent, for example. Conversely, these capacities are weakened or lost when the cohesion of the pastor's self is disturbed. Our focus throughout is on how the state of the pastor's self determines the pastor's responsiveness to time management issues in ministry. More specifically, our focus is on how the pastor can preserve his or her self-cohesion by staying "wise and affirming" so that time-related matters can be handled adequately. Time management is self-management.

LEVELS OF SELF-COHESION

Self-cohesive states exist on a continuum between "firm self-cohesion," at one end, and "weak self-cohesion," at the other. At indicated above, pastors enjoying firm self-cohesion have positive images about themselves. Their healthy self-esteem enables them to regulate the tensions they experience. They live in and through their bodies comfortably. Their thoughts are balanced and realistic. They live the time of their lives zestfully and faithfully. They face the end of their time, and the end times of loved ones, with courage. When the core of their self is threatened, by disease, loss, criticism, or rejection, for example, their cohesion is shaken but does not fall apart.

Firmly cohesive pastors also feel securely linked with

others. They respond with understanding and support. They do not patronize or try to position themselves above others. They acknowledge that all of us are children of God, who stand in need of God's loving care.

Pastors suffering from weak self-cohesion have negative images of themselves. They worry about their bodies, feel vulnerable to illness, and are physically disturbed by every criticism. They have trouble concentrating, drawing conclusions, or trusting their own sense of reality. Their publicly expressed faith feels personally empty. They live the time of their lives cautiously. They face the end of their time with fear, or with the resolve of the depressed. When faced with difficulties, they tend to withdraw or to lash out with rage.

Pastors in the extremes of weak self-cohesion also feel isolated from others. They express little sympathy and extend limited support. They may be highly suspicious. They may ward off all attempts at intimacy. They may demand perfect responses from others in order to feel secure, responding to perceived slights with rage and self-pity.

Pastors James's and Marten's present states of self-cohesion were somewhere between these extremes. Reverend James was not experiencing the most severe state of fragmentation possible for a pastor, but he was definitely unsettled. Reverend Marten was experiencing a heightened sense of well-being, but not the most profound state of personal integration possible for humans. There is a wide range of self-cohesive states between these two extremes. In our next chapter we will see more concretely how varying levels of self-cohesion produce different levels of time-management effectiveness.

FLUCTUATIONS IN SELF-COHESION

Without further information, we do not know whether James's and Marten's self-states were habitual or temporary. Reverend James's self may be chronically prone to fragmentation, or this disruption in the organization of his self may be an unusual experience for him. Self-assurance may be a basically consistent state for Reverend Marten, or it may be an exceptional peak moment in a history of otherwise personal uncertainty. Every pastor has some developmentally arrived at spot on this continuum between firm self-cohesion and weak self-cohesion.

Every pastor also experiences temporary fluctuations from his or her "normal" state of self-cohesion. Unless Reverend James's self-cohesion is chronically weak, or in the process of increased depletion, his Friday experience of fragmentation will likely pass. He will feel better about himself at some time, maybe when the sermon is completed, or when a parishioner says a good word about his preaching. Worries about himself and his abilities to handle situations will lessen, and his capacity to minister with temporal efficacy will increase.

Reverend Marten will inevitably suffer injuries to her self, resulting in some diminishing of her self-cohesion. Unless her momentary self-assurance conceals a long history of vulnerability, these injuries will not send her into deep depression. Nevertheless, she, like all of us in the ministry, is susceptible to losing her equilibrium to some degree. When that happens, her ability to be temporally attuned will also be somewhat diminished.

Fluctuations in self-cohesion are normal. The inner self-assurance of all of us vacillates. Sometimes we are more self-confident, sometimes less. Sometimes we are more securely connected to others, sometimes less. Under extreme duress, even the most self-mature of us can regress to a state of collapse. Such a condition, however, is typically momentary. We ordained ministers tend to gradually regain adequate cohesion and with it the capacities to minister well.

As a result of the vacillation of our self-cohesion, our approach to time vacillates as well. Enhanced states of self-cohesion allow us to embrace our time more intentionally. Diminished states of self-cohesion erode our capacity for living time abundantly. As indicated, in the next chapter we will see more clearly how a pastor's developmental and/or temporary state of self-cohesion markedly shapes his or her use of time.

Understanding the crucial nature of self-cohesion can be helpful to us pastors when the firmness of our self is under stress. We can be calmed by knowing what is happening to us when one day we feel on top of things and the next day we are threatened by the identical tasks. We can be fortified by realizing that our shaken state is often temporary, and that our confidence will return. We can also be sustained by a closer partnership we feel with others in ministry who all share the same inevitable disturbance of well-being.

BEING WISE AND AFFIRMING

Working to maintain healthy self-cohesion and to keep the inevitable disruptions of that cohesion at a minimum are moral responsibilities of ordained ministers. What a pastor brings to others is his or her self, and the condition of that self, for better or worse, is the agency through which ministry is accomplished. While God most certainly works wonders through us as limited, if not broken, vessels of grace, the most consistent and transforming ministry is accomplished through ministers whose self-cohesion is basically firm. Periodic or recurrent difficulties in ministry occur when the self-cohesion of the minister is enfeebled or chronically weak. Maintaining self-cohesion, therefore, is a professional and personal task of utmost importance. The term *self-management,* as we use it, means the life-long effort of the pastor to maintain basically firm self-cohesion. We are not the passive recipients of firm self-cohesion. We are called upon to act so as to contribute to our own cohesiveness.

An analogy would be our faith. Our faith is a gift to us, but we are called upon to exercise that faith, to practice and expand it. The faith given to us through God's grace is ours to nurture. If we remain passive, however, or are desperately afraid of losing the faith entrusted to us—like the steward who was afraid of losing the talent given him by the master—then we fail to grow. The same is true with our self-cohesion.

Jesus gives us guidelines for our task of self-management. In Matthew we read about the disciples who, in going out to minister, faced horrendous threats to their self-cohesion. Awaiting them, said Jesus, were humiliation, rejection, physical assault, and possibly death. In order that they might protect themselves and remain whole, Jesus fortified them with these self-saving instructions: "Be wise as serpents and innocent as doves" (Matt. 10:16).

When Jesus says, "Be wise as serpents," he is saying, "Face life shrewdly. As you go into the world, keep your head on straight." Being wise means bringing all the spiritual, psychological, and social insights we can muster to our dealings with ourself and others. Such practical wisdom involves understanding the nature of relationships, being aware of tendencies in our thinking and of the common anxieties that drive us all, and grasping the variety of ways in which, having lost our self-cohesion, we are vulnerable to being hurt and to hurting others.

Being wise with ourself includes, for example, smartening up to how the dark side of us leads to self-pity, or to berating ourself, or to acts of getting even. When our self-cohesion is threatened, we must wisely use our head. If we can do that, then our mature thoughts can take charge over that part of us that feels overwhelmed.

Being wise with others means, for example, not becoming too depressed or disillusioned when others fail to live up to our expectations. It means not being so naive as to be left with the demoralizing thought, "Well, they burst my bubble. I never thought they would do that. Life will never be the same for me again." Being wise doesn't mean being passive and nonresponsive when people disappoint us; it means not being so surprised that our self-cohesion becomes seriously shaken.

The danger in facing life wisely is that being tough-minded can lead us to become hard-hearted. Under the rationale of being healthily shrewd, we can become cynical, and thus act in ways that are harmful to others and to ourself. And so Jesus gave us the second guideline for self-management: "Be innocent as doves."

When Jesus says, "Be innocent as doves," he is saying "Face life affirmingly. As you go into the world, keep your heart straight." We are cautioned not to become so cynical that we lose the sense of goodness in others and ourself. To be affirming, however, is not just declaring a person's innate goodness. It is also the practical task of declaring that people are able to become more than they are. In affirming we say, "You are better than you think you are, and you can do more than you think you can."

Affirming others, therefore, means to avoid speaking in ways that would leave a shadow in anyone's heart. We should strive, instead, to speak in ways that fill others with a life-giving glow.

We need to affirm ourselves as pastors in that same way. Berating ourself kills our spirit even while it may prod us into greater activity. A good word to ourself is necessary, not egotistic. It reminds us that we, too, are better than we think we are, and can do more than we or others have thought we could. Affirming ourself both expresses and strengthens that wonderful feeling that an understanding, caring presence surrounds us. If God is for us, who can be against us—including ourself?

Self-cohesion is managed through the central acts of being wise and affirming with ourself and with others. Both acts are required. Wisdom without affirmation can dissipate into cynicism. We know much, but have little hope. Affirmation without wisdom, however, can result in sentimentality. We hope much, but have little effectiveness.

Being wise and affirming are pastoral attitudes. They do not spell out what to do in each situation, but how to direct ourself in ministry. To ourself, if not to others at times, we can forthrightly say, "I do not have a solution to the problem, but I do know the right attitude to take." Much of the time having the right attitude *is* the solution. Being wise and affirming are the pivotal attitudes for self-management. Guided by them, we have a better chance of maintaining our self-cohesion and responding adequately to time needs in ministry.

Chapter Two

Time Management
Dimensions in Ministry

S t. Andrew's Church was upset with their pastor. He was seldom at the church. No one could be sure when he would appear at the office. People and committees scheduled to meet him would habitually have to wait. He was always scurrying around at the last minute to get things done.

The church council as a body confronted him, demanding that he find ways to structure his time more efficiently. In an effort to bring about change, the council told their pastor that they were requiring him to take a time management course, and were strongly suggesting that he seek private counseling.

St. Andrew's advice was good, but with the wrong emphasis. Counseling should have been primary; the time management course should have been secondary. Unless their pastor is able to reliably manage his self, he will not be able to utilize time efficiency techniques with any consistency. As stated in the last chapter, the state of a pastor's self-cohesion determines the level of his or her response to time issues. A weakened self cannot be made strong simply through time organizing methods.

St. Andrew's effort to express its need was also good, but not complete. Like many other churches that suffer from inadequate ministry to their temporal needs, this congregation narrowly interpreted the problem as one of "efficiency." If only the pastor would become more efficient then presumably all would be well.

Deeper self-reflection, however, would likely reveal a wider range of temporal yearnings. For example, the congregation might realize that they hoped for a pastor who not only did things promptly but who also made time available for them personally. What they were missing, implicitly expressed in their complaint, was a pastor who showed a desire to be with them, who wanted to enter into the time of their lives in order to know and touch them. In demanding that their pastor become more efficient, they were also crying out for him to share intimately in the pains and joys of their personal histories.

Parishioners have a wide range of time needs and expectations. To minister adequately, we clergy must be aware of these temporal requirements. We must broaden our understanding of time management dimensions in ministry, and see beyond the limited time requests made by congregations. At stake is not simply our job, but also our character. We not only secure our position but we also feel better about ourself when we deal with time in mature ways. At stake also is the well-being of God's church entrusted to our care.

LEVELS OF TIME MANAGEMENT

In the last chapter we promised to show more concretely how the level of the pastor's self-cohesion shapes his or her responses to time issues in ministry. By doing that now, we also gain a picture of the various levels of time management in ministry. The following diagram not only points to the competency of the minister to handle time issues at each level of self-cohesion, but also indicates the various levels of time expectation and need parishioners have for their pastor. The latter make up those dimensions of time in ministry that clergy must manage well.

LEVELS OF SELF-COHESION	LEVELS OF TIME MANAGEMENT
COLLAPSED STATE	OWNING TIME
AMBULATORY STATE	RENDERING TIME
FUNCTIONAL STATE	USING TIME
EFFECTIVE STATE	CREATING TIME
EMPATHIC STATE	SENSING TIME
ILLUMINATIVE STATE	REVEALING TIME

Owning Time

The extreme of weakened self-cohesion is the total collapse of the pastor's self. Pastors in this state are "not doing." They are immobilized and depleted. They are unable to function. Personal hygiene may be ignored. Suicidal thoughts may be dangerously entertained.

Even if not hospitalized, these pastors abandon work at the church. Phone messages are not returned. Services are not planned. Others are left to carry out the pastor's duties.

Besides a lost capacity to structure time, pastors may also lose a sense of time. They may be unable to remember sequences of events. Hours might seem like minutes, or minutes like hours. They may have difficulty keeping track of the days of the week.

Pastors in a state of collapse may also lose their temporal continuity. They may lack the comforting feeling of being the same person they have always been. Their past may seem foreign to them. They may be unsure of who they presently are, or of what they can become.

A self-cohesive state marked by collapse can happen to any pastor given a stressful enough situation. The sudden death of a loved one may decimate the pastor. He or she may take to bed and disregard the world as grief intensifies. Such a state of severe fragmentation is usually reversible in ministry, however. As the grief is worked through, the pastor slowly regains part of her or his former self-coherence. Work is then re-engaged in a timely fashion, or at least in a fashion typical for the pastor's customary state of self-cohesion.

Congregations can be extremely understanding of wounded clergy, but they nevertheless expect a certain time management effort from them. So basic is this time management expectation that it often goes unrecognized.

Parishioners expect pastors to *own time.* Parishioners want pastors who are able to accept the hard times that befall them. They want the pastor to be able to say, "This is my life. I accept it. I make the most of it." Congregations question the guidance of pastors who try to deny or minimize the times of their lives. It is disheartening to have pastors say in the face of their personal tragedies, "I'm putting it out of my mind. I'm acting as if it didn't happen. It's not as bad as it seems."

Neither can congregations feel strengthened by pastors who stop their living dead in its track. They despair when pastors become temporally fixated, like Miss Havisham in Charles Dickens's *Great Expectations,* who lived in the ragged wedding dress she was never married in, with a moldy uneaten wedding cake nearby. At the very minimum, congregations look for pastors who are able to live robustly in the thickness of time, with all its joys and all its sorrows. They expect pastors to manage their lived time in a way that shows they own it.

Unless this happens, parishioners do not bond with pastors. Not only does the inability of pastors to own their time make them appear weak, it also alienates parishioners from them. Parishioners look for pastors who share their common lot. Only those pastors who have known and struggled through the difficulties of life are turned to for companionship and understanding when parishioners' own lives become overwhelmed. Pastors fail to present themselves as figures for comfort and guidance when they disown their time by living in the past, by minimizing the present, or by turning away fearfully from the future.

Rendering Time

One step up from the collapsed state of self-cohesion is the ambulatory state. In this condition, pastors are moving, rather than inert, but the movement is without form or direction. They are simply "doing." These pastors come to the church, but without agenda. They look at the mail, but without making any decisions about what to keep or what to throw away. A committee meeting might be attended but without any prior thought of the direction that meeting should take. These pastors are physically present but not fully present mentally or emotionally.

Although pastors in an ambulatory state may be aware of time, and may not suffer loss of temporal continuity, they do not structure time or enter into the temporal flow of church life. In their weakened state, the law of least effort prevails.

The ambulatory state of self-cohesion points to another basic time management expectation of parishioners: that the pastor will *render time*. Although congregations can be very lenient in how pastors allocate their time, they ultimately feel entitled to get what they paid for. Congregations expect pastors to devote the time they have been called to provide. "He should at least be on the job," is the underlying sentiment of parishioners, even as they tolerate for awhile the struggles of their pastor. "On the job" at the very least means the pastor being "at the job," being at the church itself "putting in his time."

Pastors often take this demand for rendering of time as an insult. They tend to feel they have a "career" rather than a "job," and that they are more like self-employed individuals who are basically free to establish their own schedules.

But time management as rendering of time is crucial in ministry. When pastors devote appropriate time to the church, that contributes to the ethos of trust congregations develop toward them. Parishioners come to trust that their pastors will honor the agreement to give them the time they have called the pastors to provide—and have paid for. More than that, parishioners come to feel securely entrusted to pastors who are, in character, honorable individuals.

When pastors are requested to keep records of the

hours they have spent and where they have been, then a serious trust problem has arisen regarding rendered time. Such requests may also be part of other problems congregations have with pastors over time management issues, such as disappointment with pastors' effectiveness. In any case, pastors minister successfully by managing time in ways that convey they are "rendering time."

Using Time

A more cohesive condition is the functional state. Here ministers are not just "doing." They are firm enough to "get things done." But what is done is minimal maintenance. Functional pastors come to church on time, get bulletins done on time, and arrange necessary meetings. The self-cohesion of these pastors, however, allows them to use time only for essential tasks that keep the church operating. There is little else beyond this.

In this functional state of self-cohesion, pastors are still expending a fair degree of their energy and time trying to hold their self together. Consequently, they are inclined to deal with easy tasks first, or to simply deal with tasks in the order in which they come. They also give priority to ridding themselves of demanding requests that further disrupt their equilibrium, rather than prioritizing time in terms of the importance of the requests.

The functional state of self-cohesion suggests another level of expected time management from ministers: *using time*. Congregations expect pastors to employ time, not just own their time or put in their time. They anticipate a minimal level of efficiency from pastors whereby order and regularity in the church is assured. Small churches served by less than adequate clergy over the years, and large churches whose membership has radically dwindled, may satisfy themselves with pastors who simply use time in ways that keep church doors open and services running. Every congregation, however, has an implicit requirement that their pastor will use time for keeping the church operationally afloat.

Adequate use of time for minimal maintenance is a comfort to parishioners. Keeping the church alive is critical for many parishioners who have made the church a center of their own cohesion. When their church closes, more than a chapter in their life story closes; their life story itself feels as though it is closing.

Furthermore, the church's regularity and order provides solace for parishioners. In more or less direct ways, they rely upon the constant rhythms and patterns of church life to provide a sense of order and regularity to their own internal life. Using time for the functional maintenance of the church is not to be disparaged; it touches the quick of those who love and lean upon the church.

Creating Time

An even firmer state of self-cohesion is the effective state. Pastors who enjoy this level of psychological integration do more than "get things done." Their firmer cohesion allows them to "get the right things done." Tasks are assigned importance. Priorities are made and acted upon. The necessity of dealing with vital but noncrisis events is recognized and addressed.

Clergy operating from an effective state are able to be more efficient than functional ministers; that is, they are able to get things done more expediently. But their most distinguishing time characteristic is their ability to employ time for activities that promote the church's growth, not merely its minimal maintenance. They are able, for example, to envision what is important for the future of the church and to work toward it. They are able to delegate maintenance tasks in order to focus time on experiences that nurture the soul of the congregation. Doing "right" things rather than "accomplishing" things is made central. Doing "right" things rather than doing "more" things is made the goal.

The self-cohesive state marked by effectiveness hints at another type of time management parishioners expect from pastors, namely *creating time*. Congregations are relieved when the church stays functional, but they are delighted when church life flows. On the one hand, parishioners look for pastors to create conditions for conserving time. Committee meetings, church projects, even worship services for some churches are enhanced when pastors keep them on track and time-contained.

There is only limited tolerance within congregations for wasted time. More and more, people in the church are impatient with what they consider nonsense. Individuals drop out of committees, and even churches, when their valuable time is frittered away. Evidence that the pastor is a good steward of time, and that events are smoothly coordinated in a right way, contributes to feelings of pleasure within the church family.

On the other hand, parishioners expect pastors to create time for activities of quality. They want to be freed up from church maintenance time so they can become involved in purposes of higher value. Pastors are expected to effectively manage so that creative time is available for parishioners. For example, an effectively run church in general creates time for extending physical and financial help to others, or for joining the denomination in world-wide projects of service and evangelism. A well-run church council meeting will create time so that council members can pray for parishioners, consider God's intentions for the congregation, or be supportive of one another. Creating time for quality involvements results in a better climate within the church, and a better feeling in the hearts of parishioners about the quality of their personal time.

Clergy need firm self-cohesion in order to adequately create time. Creating time requires the capacity to envision need, to see the bigger picture, to anticipate how things can be integrated, to stay energized for a future event, and to work with uncertainties. Inevitable blows to a pastor's self-cohesion impede the pastor's capacity to effectively create time. Once again, acknowledging this can bring soothing to both pastor and parish when the well-coordinated fabric of congregational life momentarily suffers.

Sensing Time

When pastors are in an empathic state of self-cohesion, they are attuned to the deepest yearnings of the human heart. They are able to bracket their own immediate needs and preconceptions in order to step into the subjectively lived world of others. They "walk in the other's shoes," as the old saying puts it. They empathically resonate with the stories and dreams of men, women, children, and groups. Such pastors are able to deeply listen rather than simply "do." They are able to feel with another rather than try effectively to "make things better."

Pastors with empathic self-cohesion respond thoughtfully to the temporal needs of parishioners. "I know it sounds childish," said one woman, "but I want someone to remember my birthday. I want them to call me and think of me." Empathic pastors understand these yearnings. They recall significant time-linked events in persons' lives, such as weddings, deaths, and unexpected turning points, and let these persons know they are being thought of on these anniversary dates.

Empathically capable pastors also enter into the time frames of individuals without expecting these individuals to match the timetables of others. For example, pastors will convey understanding for widows who take a lengthy time recovering from the loss of a spouse. They will show appreciation for men who make a slow emotional recovery from surgery. The uniqueness of each person's felt time and lived time is honored.

Like Reverend Marten, pastors in an empathic self-cohesive state are able to resonate with and match the time rhythms of individuals: how fast those individuals talk, think, and move. With depressed persons, ministers will be slow and deliberate. With individuals excited by a joyful event, they will act in a resonating fashion.

Similarly with groups, empathic ministers not only do the right things, they also do them at the right time. For example, they may rightly make a crisis in the church a top priority issue, but they also thoughtfully consider the time people need to integrate new information and arrive at important decisions.

Finally, empathic pastors respond understandingly when persons lose a sense of their temporal continuity. A young man recently disfigured from a car accident felt his pastor squeeze his hand and whisper, "You're still the attractive person you always were. That will never go away.

It shines from within you." His tears flowed. Someone not only appreciated him, they embraced him as the person he had always felt himself to be. Perhaps he was not now some strange figure others would be hesitant to talk to or touch. Even though his appearance was changed, maybe he still could be his old self, his old comfortable self. Empathic pastors fortify the temporal identities of traumatized souls.

Empathic self-cohesion in pastors suggests a corresponding time management expectation of parishioners, namely *sensing time*. Individuals desire pastors who are dedicated not just to saving their time, but also to sensing their time. They hope to find in the pastor one who is able to empty his or her self and enter into the lived experience of their past, present, and anticipated future. They long for pastors with warmth and understanding who can truly know what they are going through. They reach for the hand of pastors who will not judge them but will think the best of them, who will see in them those good intentions that shredded dreams and wounded pride have kept from full expression. Perhaps more than any other time management need, parishioners long for pastors to understand the time of their lives. Nothing endears a pastor to parishioners more than this.

Revealing Time

An extremely firm state of self-cohesion is marked by pastors' ability to be illuminative. Here pastors are sensitive not only to the temporal experiences of others, but also to the presence of the Transcendent in those experiences. Illuminative pastors perceive ultimate meanings in life events. They glimpse grace in the most unlikely times.

They vibrate with the awesomeness of powers beyond themselves.

In gesture and word, illuminative pastors reflect the presence and truth of God. At funerals and in worship, in pastoral calls and newsletters, they articulate with inspiring power the meaning of God having entered into our human time. Filled with the Spirit, they manifest within themselves the light of Christ. They move as spokespersons for God, not just through their calling, but by visually embodying the presence of God in the time of their life.

The illuminative state of self-cohesion points to another time management yearning of parishioners: for their pastors to *reveal time*. Parishioners turn to pastors for help in revealing the meaning of their lived time. They look for meanings that will link their inner life with their outer life, and their inner feelings with the feelings of others. Especially when their lived time is painful, or seems to have no direction, parishioners rely even more on clergy to humanize their time by finding special meaning in it.

But more than this, people turn to pastors for revelations of time that instill hope. In the long run, we all see our time against the background of our death. Time can torment us all. We are anxious about time because it reminds us of our finitude, and beckons us toward our end. Like the singer of "Old Man River," we are often "feared of livin' and scared of dyin'."

All of us at points yearn for the assurance that we will not have lived in vain. We yearn to be nurtured in a faith that can sustain us as our incarnational time decreases. Parishioners themselves lean forward in their pews hoping to hear those holy stories that link their time with God's. The pastor is that anointed one from whom people expect the fullest revealing of time's meaning.

ASSESSING SELF / TIME MANAGEMENT

This rudimentary outline of the levels of self-cohesion and time management can serve as an assessment tool for clergy. Pastors need some way to honestly appraise their present and/or habitual state of self-cohesion. Such pulse taking is part of pastors being "wise" with themselves. Ultimately it is also a means for "affirming" themselves as they periodically recall the invaluable role they have been called to live out.

Pastors can diagnose their current or habitual self-cohesive condition by considering their location on the spectrum between collapsed and illuminative states. They can verify that state more specifically by assessing how they are managing time. For example, a pastor who assumes he is in an empathic state of self-cohesion, but who consistently fails to use time effectively, has probably made a misdiagnosis about his state of self-cohesion. His self-cohesive state is likely lower than what he judges.

Pastors with developed states of empathic self-cohesion adequately fulfill time management tasks associated with their level and lower levels of self-cohesion. One does not generally find pastors in the empathic state of self-cohesion who are failing to own time, render time, use time, or create time. Empathic self-cohesive pastors, however, may lack a full capacity to reveal time. Like all of us, furthermore, they may regress periodically to lower states of self-cohesion where their higher-ordered time management capacities are briefly compromised or lost.

In the other direction, pastors in an ambulatory or functional state of self-cohesion, for example, do not fully enact the time management tasks of creating time, sensing time, or revealing time. These tasks may not be ignored, but the pastor tends to lack the self-cohesive capacities to perform them thoroughly.

Like all of us, of course, these pastors may periodically hit peak moments in self-assurance, or may permanently grow in firmness of self. As a consequence, the ground is laid for their enhanced attentiveness to creating, sensing, and revealing time.

St. Andrew's pastor could be assessed as chronically stuck in a cohesive state between ambulatory and functional. St. Andrew's complaint regarding the pastor's most glaring time deficits gives support for this assessed state of self-cohesion. The time management role St. Andrew's most clearly demanded from their pastor was a combination of rendering time and using time. They expected him to give them their due by being on location more often (rendering time). They also expected him to perform minimal functions to keep the church operative (using time). As indicated previously, however, St. Andrew's most likely carried in its corporate heart other time needs, although these were not clearly articulated.

Assessment confusion arises when time management efforts are looked at without due consideration for the self-cohesive state from which these time efforts originate. The meaning of a pastor's time efforts takes on clarity when understood from the viewpoint of his or her prevailing state of self-cohesion.

As a common example, a pastor's concentrated attention on effective time management does not necessarily indicate a pastor with firm self-cohesion. In an attempt to block off disturbing feelings of self-doubt, the pastor may become engrossed in matters of organization and effectiveness. She anticipates, more or less consciously, that this activity of being on top of things will energize her and boost her self-esteem. Scheduling, structuring, making charts, revamping committees, streamlining the office and all other "time efficiency" efforts are used to hold the beleaguered self of the pastor together. Even when the pastor's self-cohesion is not immediately endangered, she may overachieve in order to establish an image that can be relied upon to save her when pressures threaten her reputation.

Parishioners close to the scene discern that the pastor is "trying too hard." She cannot relax. Disruptions disturb her. In this situation the cleric tends to keep an extraordinarily tight rein on things, and to build up elaborate rationalizations for what is done. Over time, congregations become aware that these projects for efficiency serve more the pastor's needs than theirs.

Time management efforts, therefore, can become a way for overcoming a weakened sense of competence. Strict adherence to time matters may function for the pastor as a means for self-coherence. Time management efforts may become *the* means used by the pastor for attempting to dispel feelings of self-doubt and ineffectiveness. While these time efforts may actually benefit the church, they do not necessarily represent a pastor with firm self-cohesion. The state of the clergyperson's self determines the nature of time management endeavors.

ULTIMATE PURPOSE OF TIME MANAGEMENT

In *Alice in Wonderland,* the Mad Hatter says, "If you knew time as well as I do, you wouldn't talk about wasting *it.* It's *him.*" The Hatter is pointing to the lived essence of time. Time is personal. It is intrinsically part of who we are. When we talk about time we are not ultimately talking about an "it," a quantity like water that is outside of us that we can use or waste. Time is us. What gets used or wasted is the time of our life. If we substitute the word "life" for the word "time" in the phrases "I'm losing time," "I haven't found the time," or "I don't know where time went," then we are closer to appreciating what time is all about: "I'm losing life," "I haven't found the life," "I don't know where life went."

Time management, therefore, is not ultimately about time; it is about people. Time management has to do with affecting the lives of others. How we deal with time in ministry does not incidently or secondarily affect people; how we deal with time *is* dealing with people.

Time management is a process that organizes not just activities, but also experiences. It is a meaning-giving process, not a neutral process. Whether setting up office hours, or reorganizing a church committee, or drawing up new church bylaws, or devoting time to calling on families, every time management effort is attached to individual selves who need to feel understood. There is a heart attached to each time management decision. A decided impact upon the self-cohesion of individual parishioners, therefore, and upon the self-cohesion of the church as a group, is made with each time management effort or lack thereof.

For example, when a pastor decides to use the secretary more efficiently by setting up an automated answering system that begins, "Dial one if you want . . . , dial two if you want . . . ," there is an "end of time" for some parishioners, a sense that the church is always personally there and personally concerned has ended. "It's over. It's no longer as it was." And with this ending of a time comes a sense of loss, and with this loss, as with all losses, some disturbance of the person's self-cohesion.

Other time management decisions are experienced positively. They are taken either as the "end of time" of something atrocious, or as the "beginning of a new time" of something rewarding. Here, too, how the pastor deals with time issues affects the subjective time of parishioners and the firmness or weakness of their self-cohesion.

All this leads up to the most appropriate manner in which to regard time. *The ultimate purpose of time management in the church should be to preserve, restore, and consolidate the self-cohesion of others.* The goal of a pastor's use of time should be to contribute to the wellness of selves.

This moral assertion is necessary. Time management can be used for a host of objectives that disregard the needs of people. When time management moves are made without moral guidance, that is, employed for purposes other than contributing to the wholeness of selves, then such moves can prove detrimental. Pastors can manage time in order to control others, or to keep their empire within the church afloat, or to elevate their reputation, or to hide their crimes. A call to be "life enhancing" is desecrated when "time" becomes an impersonal substitute for "life," and "management" becomes a manipulative replacement for "enhancing." Although it may seem extreme, unless time efficiency methods are linked with the moral purpose of keeping people whole, they can be as dangerous as teaching others to shoot a gun without knowing what they intend to shoot.

The content of the following pages is structured by the clinical observation that self-management shapes time management, and by the moral premise that pastors have a responsibility to work toward the maintenance of their self-cohesion through being "wise and affirming." The moral assertion in this chapter, that the ultimate purpose of time management should be the maintenance of self-cohesion in others, does not give structure to our following chapters. But it pervades all that is said. Ultimately, pastors fail to be "wise and affirming" unless they acknowledge this moral call.

Chapter Three

Self/Time Management

in Pastoral Care

Reverend Marten recognized the voice of the un-identified caller. Although she was barely awake, she knew it was the parishioner whom she had consoled six months earlier, along with his two children, at the hospital. But she could not make out the words. He was sobbing uncontrollably. She caught something about his not being able to get over it, about having wrecked the house in anger, and about not being a good father.

Her heart suddenly clutched. Were the girls there? she asked. Were they all right? Through his garbled response she made out a no. No *what*, she came back stronger, no not there or no not all right? No they were not there, but he had not been a good dad to them.

Her heart eased, then raced again. Had he been so upset that he had been thinking of suicide? she asked. He paused. No, not really. But what about now? Was he feeling suicidal now? The voice on the other end sobered a bit. No, he was just feeling overwhelmed. Could she come over right away?

Taking a deep breath she said that she knew he was feeling lonely and scared, and that he needed the comfort of others around him, but she suggested that he simply turn out the lights and go to bed, and in the morning meet with her at the church. Would he come? At 9:30 A.M.? Yes, he said. But why couldn't she come now? She was his pastor, wasn't she? He was really in bad shape. Wasn't it her job to help people when they needed it? She reassured him that she cared, and that she knew he was disappointed, but that she could be of greater help to him in the morning.

Reverend Marten's hand was not steady as she replaced the phone. Had she done the right thing? What if the situation became worse? Could she really be of greater help in the morning?

She now felt overwhelmed herself. Her breathing was short. Her mind reeled. Although she did not like to admit it, she was angry at her caller. He should be coping better with his grief, she thought disgustedly, rather than upsetting everyone, including her, with his immature reactions.

She shook her head to clear the thought away. Maybe she should follow her own advice: simply turn off the lights and get some rest. In the morning she would have to think about how to keep herself calm as she tried to help him and the girls. She pulled the covers tight and closed her eyes, hoping her imitation of sleep would hasten its reality.

SELF-COHESION AND PASTORAL CARE

Pastoral care is dangerous. The self-cohesion of pastors is ceaselessly threatened by the pain of parishioners. Although pastors hear joyful news, most often they hear peoples' anguished stories. Those stories not only tire pastors, they trouble them.

The self-cohesion of pastors is also threatened by their own reactions. Although the very best in pastors can be called forth, pastoral care relations elicit their deepest anxieties and defenses. These responses often increase fragmentation rather than curtail it. As a result, the well-being of both parishioners and pastors is diminished rather than enhanced.

Reverend Marten's nighttime experience illustrates how the firm self-cohesion of any pastor can be unexpectedly shaken. We clergy get caught off-guard, and thus knocked off-center. That loss of cohesion may be momentary, just a few minutes, or it may linger, even though we have felt confident about our previous pastoral care efforts. We may begin to doubt ourselves. We may begin to have negative feelings about those who lean on us for help.

In either case, lost self-cohesion leads to loss of time. We may spend an inordinate amount of time trying to reassure ourselves. We may withdraw into periods of self-comfort, or we may throw ourselves into the specific problem that has threatened our self-esteem. These responses are understandable, but not viable, solutions.

Pastors need to be wise and affirming when dealing with parishioners and themselves in the ministry of pastoral care. If clergy disregard these efforts at self-management, their self-cohesion will be jeopardized. As a consequence, their responses to the time needs of parishioners will tend to be less than adequate. Time management requires self-management, the maintenance of self-cohesion through the directing attitudes of being wise and affirming.

We clergy need God's help in trying to stay wise and affirming in the activity of pastoral care. Our wisdom requires a surrender to the guidance and corrections of God. We must confess profusely that we "know only in part." In each act of pastoral care we beseech God not only to grant us wisdom, but also to bring healing through those times when we have been unwise.

Our efforts to be affirming rely upon seeing in the face of every woman and man the face of Jesus who says, "I died for this person." Every individual, including the pastor, is struggling with more conflicts and troubles than others ever realize, and every individual is eternally cared for by their Creator, who will never let them go. The burden of affirming, which affirming can be, is made easier by the knowledge of God's unconditional love for us all.

BEING WISE ABOUT OURSELF

Being wise about ourself is not easy. A part of us resists knowing what we already suspect about our actions and motives. Nonetheless, healthy self/time management in the ministry of pastoral care necessitates that we monitor our guilt, our reactions to criticisms, and our need to feel special.

Monitoring Guilt

Evidence suggests that some pastors deflect the guilt they feel in pastoral care relationships. For example, incidents in which pastors become sexually involved with parishioners under their care do not point to a lack of conscience. These pastors often experience guilt. They feel remorse and have misgivings, during and after these involvements. Unfortunately they do not always wisely respond to that guilt.

In various ways these clergy shun their guilt. They push it away as too difficult to deal with, or rationalize that the situation was "not that bad." They minimize the guilt by privately claiming to themselves that love and good intentions were involved, or that one is "only human," or that it was only an "isolated instance."

All the while, the very core of their self is in severe danger. The stable integration of their beliefs, self-control, and empathy is weakened or lost. Their sexual involvement with parishioners indicates that their self-cohesion is fragmenting.

Guilt, however, goes unheeded. Guilt as God's way of calling us back to wholeness, guilt as our alarm system alerting us to the real or potential disintegration of our self, is essentially ignored. By failing to respond wisely to healthy guilt, pastors fail to grasp an opportunity for redemption. As a result, pastors' precious self-cohesion, and that of the parishioners they abuse, becomes more imperiled.

Time is eroded when pastors do not heed their guilt. Pastors may squander church and family time by daydreaming about parishioners, for example. Reliving the moments of excitement with a parishioner, or fantasizing about a full-blown romantic-sexual relationship, crowd out productive hours. Pastors may waste inordinate amounts of time in pseudo-pastoral care that is essentially flirtatious, voyeuristic, or controlling. Time is siphoned away from necessary tasks as pastors mull over how to minimize being exposed or what line of defense they would use if accused.

Wise pastors perceive that when guilt is deflected, judicious use of time is thwarted. Pastors who minimize their guilt are not owning their own time. They are not living in the present moment. They are not facing courageously the meaning of their past, present, and future. They may not be adequately rendering or using time as they become embroiled in defending themselves against exposure, or against recognizing their culpability. Wise responses to the promptings of guilt can preserve the self-cohesion of pastors and the fullness of time they are given to use and enjoy.

Monitoring Criticisms

Criticisms hurt. Even when offered by well-meaning parishioners, or requested by pastors themselves, criticisms disturb pastors' self-cohesion. One seasoned pastor said, "After all these years, I'm still more sensitive to being criticized than I am to not being praised." The more insecure the pastor, the more threatening the criticisms. A pastor who had been fired from his previous church admitted that even the slightest criticism both stung and alarmed. "I'm both hurt and scared at the same time whenever I hear a negative word."

Wise clergy keep their reactions to criticisms in check. When confronted with a disapproving comment about their pastoral care, they ask themselves two simultaneous questions: "What is it about me that elicited that comment? What is it about the other that made them say it?" Astute pastors try to benefit from whatever truth about themselves the criticism might contain. At the same time they reflect on how the criticism may be a sign of what is happening in the life of the critic. A healthy balance between openness to correction and consideration of the source is established. As a result of this self-management, self-cohesion is preserved and pastoral care efforts stay vital.

When criticisms are not properly considered, they can

erode a pastor's self-cohesion. As confidence dwindles, criticisms are responded to personally. Specific complaints are taken as general indictments. Concern for others gives way to anxious withdrawal. Retaliatory acts rather than reconciling acts fill the mind.

As pastors lose their capacity for self-management in the face of criticism, they lose the capacity for adequate time management in pastoral care. A pastor may curtail pastoral care efforts, for example. Out of hurt or bitterness, the pastor may render only the bare minimum of time with grieving families, or make home visits only when called upon, or refer everyone who comes for counseling. Sharing the time of life with parishioners is minimized.

Criticism-sensitive pastors may also withdraw into a formal pastoral care stance. To defend against reproach, these pastors do everything "by the book." They surround themselves with pastoral procedures and structured pastoral acts. Established policies for home visitation, funerals, and hospital calling are set forth. For example, a pastor announced to the church council that hospital calls would be routinely made on Tuesdays and Fridays. All other requests for hospital visitations were to be made through the church secretary. Each hospital call would be approximately fifteen minutes, and would include a scripture reading and prayer.

With this approach everything was done with order. Unfortunately it was also done without a relaxed, understanding spirit. "I make pastoral care just a job that I do. I don't let myself get caught up with feelings," he stated. Attempting to preserve his self-cohesion by assuming a formal pastoral care stance, this pastor spent significant time making sure he followed procedures and conveyed them clearly to parishioners. Maintenance of the structure rather than ministry to persons becomes central. Time management for activities replaced time management for relationships. Time was dispensed quantitatively, based on the pastoral task rather than the personal need.

In the face of criticisms, clergy may also expend large amounts of time in self-scrutiny. They may fret not only about strong individuals becoming angry at them, but also about weak individuals becoming disappointed in them. Pastors may spend restless nights and worry-riddled days wondering if they said the wrong thing at a funeral, or acted caringly enough at the hospital, or had bad breath and gave bad advice in counseling, or were not sufficiently religious during a home visitation.

Self-scrutiny easily leads to self-pity. Pastors may spend increased time licking their wounds and comforting themselves in ways they feel others could never do. As self-pity deepens, so does the loss of self-cohesion. Becoming more and more anxious about criticisms, pastors may teeter on the brink of collapse, where they are unable to own their own time, or to render time to parishioners.

Monitoring Needs for Specialness

Wise pastors monitor their need to feel special. The pastor's chest can swell as parishioners convey how wonderful he or she has been. These reassurances can be blessings. In healthy circumstances, such affirmations sustain a pastor's good feelings about himself or herself, and help heal injuries that have been suffered.

Pastoral care, however, can be an elixir. For those pastors suffering from weakened self-cohesion, pastoral care may provide the means for experiencing the high of being special. Feeling indispensable to parishioners, or hearing accolades from them, may become an addictive antidote for their persistent self-doubts. As a result, these pastors hunger for situations in which they can be elevated into grand caretaker status. Church administration, preaching, or family life may be shortchanged in preference for any form of pastoral care in which the pastor feels wanted and needed.

Enormous amounts of time may be given to these pastoral care endeavors. "We tried to tell our minister that we appreciated all the time he was spending at the hospital, but that he also needed to spend more time in the office on administrative matters," relayed one council member. "He accused us of not being sensitive to him or to those in need. It's not that. It's just that he seems preoccupied with going to the hospital and making calls on those who are sick."

Pastors may also spend significant time *creating* pastoral care opportunities for themselves. For instance, they may establish multiple groups in the church that meet supposedly different needs: groups for those newly divorced, for those with physical ailments, for those with addictions, or for those out of work. These groups may be formed out of the pastor's need to feel special, rather than to fill requests from others. While the groups may eventually prove beneficial to some parishioners, specialness-hungry pastors tend to move on to new groups when established groups fail to stimulate the pastor's self-esteem.

In a similar way pastors may look for crisis situations. Some pastors experience not only a firmer sense of who they are during a crisis, but also an excited sense of being special. Consequently, while these pastors may not create crises in order to elevate their self-esteem, they may be more ready to declare a situation a crisis than to dismiss it as a flare-up. A crisis management approach may be used in nearly every pastoral care situation as a means for the pastor to shine. As we know too well, parish life-time is inevitably sucked up in the black holes of crises. Unfortunately, some pastors contribute to those black holes.

Thoughtful pastors recognize their needs to feel special, especially when their self-cohesion is low or threatened. They are aware of how disproportionate amounts of time devoted to activities like pastoral counseling or hospital visitation can be used to stimulate self-esteem. Wise ministers want to feel special, too, of course. They just go about it with greater maturity. The first step is monitoring the need.

BEING WISE ABOUT OTHERS

Being wise about ourselves as pastors is perhaps more important than being wise about others. It is at least more humbling. How others act toward us as clergy does influence our state of self-cohesion, however. We also maintain our self-cohesion and our effective use of time in ministry by pastoral management of parishioners' emergencies and selfobject expectations.

Managing Emergencies

True emergencies are rare. Calls for pastoral help are usually the result of long-standing problems that suddenly upset parishioners. Even calls announcing that someone has died, or is dying, are not emergencies strictly speaking.

Calls are frequently an emergency for the callers, however. The stressful event causes them anxiety. Rather than respond to that anxiety as a "signal" that something must be attended to, they tend to respond with "alarm." The event becomes a crisis. Near panic ensues. Quick responses from pastors are expected or demanded.

While pastors should be thoughtful of these sudden disturbances of parishioners' self-cohesion, they can wisely remember that very little is actually a 7.0 on the Richter scale of seriousness. Insightful clergy respond to calls with signal anxiety rather than alarm anxiety. While they sense the time-urgency of parishioners, they themselves do not become frantic. They recognize that a response is needed, but not with the speed or intensity dictated by an actual life-and-death situation.

Emergency-wise pastors, therefore, spend time thinking through the most fitting response to parishioners, rather than reacting in a knee-jerk way. Reverend Marten's decision not to rush over to her parishioner's house in the dead of night was based upon a quick assessment that things there were serious but not dangerous. She also knew that pastoral matters could become complicated if she, a female clergyperson, visited a lonely, distressed male parishioner all alone. She understood, furthermore, that when pastors move at a calm, balanced pace, they are better able to convey peacefulness to anxious parishioners. Life-time regains a sense of normal flow for laity as pastors maintain their own equilibrium.

Emergency-wise pastors will be more inclined to offer time approaches to persons in crisis. Cohesive pastors frame parishioners' time rather than try to instantly solve their anxious problems. Reverend Marten, for instance, recommended a respite period to her parishioner, namely that he cease his self-rebuke and destructive acts by going to bed. The old joke about the physician's ubiquitous prescription for every ailment ("Take two aspirin and call me in the morning") contains sage advice. Getting rest and seeing how things are in the light of a new day can change crisis reactions into common unhappiness.

Pastors can also structure time for persons who feel in crisis. For example, when a husband and wife come to the pastor for counseling, ragefully declaring that the other is impossible to live with and that a divorce is the only solution, the pastor can suggest a moratorium. "You are too caught up in anger and hurt to make a wise decision. You need to set aside a time period where you do not talk about divorce or seek advice from a lawyer, but begin to reflect on the causes that brought you to this point." A structured time period itself does not cure, but it does make possible the deintensification of the crisis and the emergence of healing processes.

Similarly, a pastor may suggest a "forty-eight-hour rule" to family members in conflict. The pastor may say: "This family keeps too many things bottled up, which come out later when a specific problem arises. Everyone is afraid of saying anything, because they're worried it will come back to haunt them. So I'm suggesting a forty-eight-hour rule. If you have a beef with someone, you've got to talk to that person within a forty-eight-hour period, or else you have to forget it. No more hanging on to things for days or weeks." Time directives such as these help parishioners reclaim the quality of their lived time. Much, however, depends upon pastors' wise understanding of the nature of emergencies.

Managing Selfobject Expectations

Pastors have no autonomy, psychologically speaking. Parishioners do not basically react to pastors as if pastors were separate from them. While they know that pastors have individual lives and private thoughts, at the most basic emotional level parishioners experience pastors as part of them. Pastors are responded to as "selfobjects," as objects attached to and part of the self of each parishioner.[1]

As selfobjects, pastors are not simply depended upon. They are experienced as extensions of the life of parishioners. Ministers' pastoral care responses are expected to come when parishioners want them to come, and in the form parishioners want them to come. When pastors fail to provide adequate selfobject responses, parishioners tend to respond with varying degrees of anger or withdrawal.

For example, when Reverend Marten's parishioner called late at night, he expected her to be there for him. His shaken state was not the cause of his disregard for her sleep, or of his irritation when she would not come over. He, like all parishioners more or less, responded to his pastor as his selfobject, as a person he expected to be for him as he needed. The disintegration of his self-cohesion only made his selfobject expectations more blatant. They came out more primitively. But they were always there.

They were there, for instance, immediately after his wife died. He reached out to Reverend Marten, looking for her to comfort and sustain him when he was not able to do that himself. He expected that she would understand, that she would always stand by him and the girls, and that she would make herself available to him as the need arose. At the hospital she was able to meet his selfobject needs, in part because his selfobject requests at that time were simple and appropriate.

Selfobject expectations are normal. The most basic psychological way we all relate to others is as our selfobjects.

We all need to experience that others are for us, with us, part of us. We feel reassured when others fulfill the roles we have expected of them. We feel confident when others give themselves to us, making our goals theirs, embracing our values as theirs. We feel soothed when people seem to know our needs and help us satisfy them. Parishioners bring their normal selfobject expectations to their relationship with their pastor.

The more fragile the self-cohesion of parishioners, however, the more they rely upon the pastor to fill their selfobject expectations. The more vulnerable the self-cohesion of a congregation as a group, the more that group will insist on certain behavior from the pastor in order to feel safe. Selfobject needs of parishioners can be immature, if not pathological. When pastors respond inadequately to these excessive selfobject needs, parishioners' reactions of anger and withdrawal intensify.

For instance, when one pastor expressed his theological understanding about open and closed caskets to a family making funeral arrangements in his office, he was later reprimanded in a special church council meeting. "The family was very upset by what you said," exclaimed the church moderator in front of those gathered. "You're being paid a lot of money to suck up to people, and you're not doing your job." The pastor was not regarded as a person, not even as a leader, but as a mere selfobject expected to fulfill a prescribed function. He was relegated to being a hired hand, one whose selfobject chore—sucking up to people and making them feel good no matter what—violated his pastoral and personal integrity. His integrity, however, was not as important as the function they expected him to perform.

Wise clergy try to pastorally manage the selfobject

needs of parishioners. They realize, on the one hand, how normal selfobject expectations require much time. "Surely the minister will visit our sick aunt, even though she is not a member." "Surely the minister has time to come to our house." "Surely the minister will see to it that special arrangements are made for the funeral." Much of pastoral care is taken up by typical parishioners looking for those special responses from the pastor they expect will be there as they need them.

Pastors also recognize, on the other hand, how parishioners with excessive selfobject needs absorb whatever pastoral and personal time they can extract from their clergy. Individuals may try to stay in constant contact with their pastors, calling them on the phone, or making sure to seek them out on a Sunday morning to convey how they feel. Other individuals may carry on campaigns against a pastor who may have injured them in some way. As a result, the pastor expends valuable time trying to minimize the damage caused by the disgruntled parishioners.

Wise pastors set empathic boundaries. They try to express understanding for the selfobject needs of parishioners while yet setting limits on how those needs are met. Reverend Marten, for example, expressed understanding for her parishioner's yearning for her presence late at night, but she maintained her boundaries. She also empathically offered to see him later, but in a situation with appropriate boundaries, namely her office at the church. If Reverend Marten's distraught parishioner had wanted to stay in her office with her for hours, Reverend Marten would have needed to express empathic understanding for his yearning to feel in a safe place while yet setting limits on that meeting's length. If he had stated that he wanted to come back to see her every day that week, she, again, would have needed to empathically resonate with his feelings but structure the number of times they met.

Pastors must also find ways to set empathic boundaries on the selfobject rage of disgruntled parishioners. Whatever strategies pastors and supportive church leaders devise to deal with these unhappy members, pastors must always keep their pastor hat on. That is, pastors should always respond to disruptive parishioners as God's children, and always respond to troubles they generate as pastoral problems. These individuals and the difficulties they cause are not exceptions to what pastors are called to face in the church. They are part of the very stuff of individual and communal life standing in need of redemption. Pastors maintain empathic boundaries by staying in their pastoral role.

What parishioners ultimately want is to feel understood. If the pastor can empathically express understanding for their needs and wishes, even though the pastor may not fulfill them the way parishioners want, parishioners may react with disappointment rather than withdrawal, or with annoyance rather than rage.

Wise pastors realize, however, that no matter how empathic they are, no matter how much time they give to persons with pressing selfobject needs, it is never enough. Parishioners with pressing selfobject needs have a psychic hole in their toe. It does not matter how much time and attention the pastor pours into them, it keeps running out and they turn to the pastor for more.

If pastors do not adequately manage the selfobject expectations/demands of parishioners, the self-cohesion of pastors themselves becomes weakened. When the pastor is constantly expected to empty himself or herself for the needs of parishioners, the self-cohesion of the pastor loses firmness and vitality. Symptoms of burnout often arise when pastors repetitively give themselves to the typical and excessive pastoral care expectations of parishioners. Like Jesus, who became overwhelmed by the demands of the crowd around him, pastors, too, often want to flee. The informed pastor, therefore, tries to empathically manage parishioners' selfobject needs.

AFFIRMING OURSELF

In a recent survey of pastors conducted by Fuller Seminary, 70 percent reported having a lower self-image than when they started ministry.[2] That's an unsettling statistic. How can we account for it? My own counseling of pastors suggests two causes. In the first place, selfobject demands of parishioners take their toll. The self-image of pastors is lowered when they fail to receive thoughtful affirmations from parishioners they serve, and when their very integrity is undercut by disgruntled laity.

In the second place, pastors tend to be ineffective in affirming themselves. Young pastors typically enter ministry with idealistic expectations, if not grandiose self-images. They expect to win souls for Christ, to heal broken hearts, and to be loved by their congregations. That lived-for scenario rarely becomes incarnate. Lacking a capacity to realistically sustain their own self-esteem over time and difficulties, their fractured dreams cast up dismal self-images.

Older individuals entering ministry either have learned to support themselves during rough times or else experience an intensification of those negative self-images they hoped ministry would cure. When the latter happens, these pastors, like their young colleagues, also lose their self-cohesion and their effective use of time in ministry. Whether old or young, there is a nostalgia for good feelings in pastors, which healthy affirmations from themselves and from others can resurrect.

Affirming One's Doing

Clergy spend considerable time thinking about the results of their work rather than about their work itself. They focus on the success or failure of their pastoral ministry. They keep numerical records of increases or decreases in attendance and of requests for pastoral help. They assess the impact of their pastoral care on others, and justify their ministry by the consequences they produce: growth in members, increased giving, more participation, happier parishioners. Unfortunately "results" is the wrong priority, and the wrong basis, for self-esteem.

Pastors recover positive self-images when they affirm the value of their doing rather than its fruits. They tend to stay even-minded when they are moved less by concerns for success or failure and more by the value of their pastoral work. While recognizing the importance of results, pastors benefit from not making them primary. "I'm in a lot better shape when I keep reminding myself that what I do has worth," said one pastoral counselor. "When I slip and let my self-esteem rise or fall based on how many clients I have, or how much they are paying, or how many calls I get to lead seminars, then I'm in trouble. My sense of worth is more stable when I affirm that my work itself is worthwhile, no matter what."

When a pastor takes it as a personal rejection when her pastoral calls on people do not result in their increased church attendance, then the basis of her worth is misplaced. When a pastor becomes despondent because his Bible study group attracts only faithful members and not new faces, then the basis of his worth is also misplaced. When clerics judge the value of their pastoral efforts by the amount they are compensated by the church, then the basis of their self-esteem is dangerously situated. Pastoral care of people is a pearl of great price, and not a means for what it can gain pastors or how it can make them appear to others. When Jesus said, "Truly I tell you, just as you did it to one of the least of these who are members of my family, you did it to me" (Matt. 25:40), Jesus was not talking of pastoral results. He was talking about the value of having a pastoral heart. Care doing is Christ-like. Pastors maintain self-esteem by affirming their worth in the holy acts of their pastoral care.

When pastors are able to affirm themselves in their work, they are infused with generic positive feelings. They feel relaxed, calm, and enthused. They live their own life-time more fully, and enter the lived time of parishioners in a self-forgetting way. "When I embraced myself and my work again, I felt I was on track with a lot of things," expressed a previously failure-anxious pastor. "I experienced a sense of self-forgetfulness that did not harm me and made me more open to others and able to hear them." Self-affirmation contributes to firm self-cohesion, whereby clergy need not expend personal or parish time ruminating about their reputation or the prospects of failure. Self-affirmation is time effective.

Establishing Self-Affirmations

When pastors experience the loss of self-cohesion, they look for soothing. Without established self-affirming rituals or thoughts, pastors spend time casting about for something that will restore their self-esteem. Quality of life as well as time is preserved when pastors have at hand self-affirming rituals or thoughts that bring reassurance.

For example, one pastor found comfort in this self-affirming litany: "I'm better than I think I am and I can do more than I think I can. I'm better than I think I am and I can do more than I think I can." He took that as God's message to him. He gave the words a rhythm, a beat, that along with the thought pulsed through him soothingly. Another pastor found solace kneeling before the altar in the darkened church, repeating aloud, and slowly, the Twenty-third Psalm. His spirit was infused with hope again as he closed with the glorious words, "Surely goodness and mercy shall follow me all the days of my life; and I shall dwell in the house of the LORD for ever" (Ps. 23:6 RSV).

Self-affirming rituals and thoughts vary among clergy. Each one is valid as long as it is not a substitute for resolving problems, or does not undercut communal life with others. Stated pragmatically, established self-affirmations are part of clergy's self/time management.

AFFIRMING OTHERS

The affirming responses of others are the foundation of an individual's stable and coherent sense of self. At the same time, gloriously enough, the *giving* of affirming responses contributes to the giver's stable and coherent sense of self. Acts of affirmation bless both the receiver and the sender. Affirming others, therefore, is an invaluable part of pastors' own self-affirmation. Thinking well of parishioners sustains pastors' self-cohesion. As a result it also allows them to deal appropriately with time issues in the ministry.

Affirming Subjective Truth

Parishioners, like all persons, have their individual views of reality, their particular ways of experiencing themselves and the life around them. When the felt truth of their experiences is challenged or dismissed by others, then parishioners' hold on their reality is shaken. They become uncertain about what they know, about what they should do, and about what they can hope. Their self-cohesion is threatened, if not fragmented.

Conversely, parishioners feel affirmed when they feel believed. Their self-cohesion is strengthened when pastors honor them by validating their subjective truth. When, for example, a grieving widow says to her pastor, "My life is over," the empathic pastor resonates with and shows understanding for her present subjective truth. The pastor will not say, "You don't really mean that," or "That's just a passing phase." Instead the pastor will understand that for this woman at this moment her time *has* ended. Her past is gone. Her familiar present is no more. Her future is foreclosed. And so the pastor may say, "With his death something inside you has died too." That affirmation of her subjective truth begins her journey toward new life. As she and other parishioners feel understood by the pastor, their collapsed selves slowly regain cohesion.

Affirming the subjective truth of others also preserves clergy's own self-cohesion. Not only does the act of being empathic generate positive self-feelings within pastors, but pastors are also better able to endure the moods and behaviors of parishioners by acknowledging the truth of their truth. Internal frustration is minimized when pastors affirm that all persons strive to construct a reality tolerable to themselves and reassuringly consistent with their experiences. Empathy for parishioners is extended when pastors affirm that all persons are doing the best they can as they try to find meaning in, and to give meaning to, their self and their relationships.

When pastors affirm subjective truth they are using time effectively. Pastoral care interventions foster healing when they are guided by an understanding of parishioners' lived reality. Pastors have to first accept the truth of parishioners because only through accepting it can pastors understand the meaning of it. Once they understand, they can then empathically respond. When pastors try to circumvent this process by combating parishioners' subjective truth, or by imposing their own meaning on parishioners' experience, they waste time. Their presence fails to promote soothing. Their words fail to promote insight. Their misguided procedure misuses pastoral time. More importantly, it misuses the life-time of parishioners, who wait, often silently, for an understanding word that affirms the truth in their suffering. Affirming parishioners' subjective truth supports pastors' self/time management in pastoral care, allowing them to be more effective channels of God's grace to others.

Validating Intentions

When parishioners lose their self-cohesion, they are more inclined to act in ways hurtful to themselves and others. In the midst of this, they long to feel understood and to have others think well of them. They yearn for others to know that their intentions are good, even though their actions at the moment do not match those intentions.

Pastors affirm parishioners when they validate their good intentions. "I know you have a loving heart and would do anything for your children," said Reverend Marten to her parishioner the next morning. What he needed at that point was not a pastoral lecture about doing his duty or changing his behavior. He needed to be reminded of his goodness, and to hear that others still thought well of him. To have lost the image that others affirmed him would have been to lose the motivation to reclaim his life. Reverend Marten's affirmation of his good intentions had the potential of drawing him back to his best self. It would fortify his self-cohesion so that he could fight the good fight and become the man he knew in his heart he could be.

Affirming the good intentions in parishioners also protects the self-cohesion of pastors. When parishioners act in harmful ways, to one another and to their pastors, clergy sustain themselves by remembering the good beneath the bad. "Several times a day I have to keep reminding myself that people are created in the image of God and that they are created good," said one pastor. "If I start to feel that people are basically a sinful, selfish lot, then I begin to act surly toward them. I become guarded, cool, and more ready to lay down the law than offer a good word." Affirming good intentions protects pastors from becoming contaminated by the evil that does exist.

Cohesive pastors who think the best of parishioners serve the best. In the first place, fortified by having affirmed good intentions, pastors can give healing time to parishioners who are the least likable, for that is when they need that time the most. In the second place, a pastoral care model based on created goodness is more effective than a model based on sin and sickness. People grow toward the pictures they and others have of them. They fulfill the images and expectations they and others hold about who they are and what they will become.

Parishioners' selves, consequently, are shaped by the attitudes pastors take toward them in pastoral care. When pastors view parishioners positively, and when every word and act expresses a vision of parishioners living their fullest and best selves, then parishioners are moved to become the selves God created them to be. Confronting parishioners or calling them to accountability are restorative acts when they express to parishioners the pastor's high regard for who they are and who they can be. Self/time management is most effective in pastoral care when pastors work from an approach that affirms parishioners' good intentions and their yearnings for wholeness.

Chapter Four

Self/Time Management

in Preaching

For the third time Reverend James's fingers reached for the delete keys. The screen on his word processor became instantly blank again, except for the ever-present cursor, whose relentless blinking reminded him of the passing, and wasting, of time.

He was pushing for something to come. He hoped that a good first line would give him direction, that it would inspire him to helpfully apply the Scripture reading to the life of the congregation. A swirl of half-formulated thoughts buzzed in his head like erratic flies without a coordinated purpose.

For some reason, images from a video he had watched the night before came flooding in. The movie had impressed him. There were obvious religious overtones in it, but Reverend James wasn't certain about the religious message, or how it might fit with the Scripture lessons for that Sunday, or even how the congregation might react. Let it go, he thought. Better to be safe than sorry.

But he wasn't feeling safe, and he certainly *was* feeling sorry for himself. This whole preaching process should be easier, he said to himself. It shouldn't take so much out of him each week. Aware that he was slipping into self-pity, he tried to refocus his thinking. Just get the job done, he directed himself, and without looking up at the cursor he typed his fourth opening line.

SELF-COHESION AND PREACHING

Preaching threatens the self-cohesion of pastors more than any other pastoral duty. Pastoral care is often private, and often with just one or a few related parishioners at a time. Church administration is frequently declared a shared responsibility between clergy and laity. But in the pulpit pastors stand alone, and in front of all. Few pastors experience "preaching with the congregation," or having the congregation as a "partner" in preaching. Psychologically, and in terms of parishioners' expectations, preaching is the pastor's. Furthermore, although there are multiple dimensions to a pastor's work, if a congregation should be weakened or collapse, the sword in its heart is often declared to be the sermon.

Few preachers are immune to the rush of adrenalin that comes from anticipating either praise or criticism. "After thirty years in the ministry, I still get butterflies when the sermon hymn comes to a close and I have to step in the pulpit. Sometimes I feel that I have something new to say, something important that I think will illuminate their minds and bring hope. I get excited about that. Other times I feel that I'm in a rut, simply repeating Sunday after Sunday the same old lines. And I imagine that they're as bored with me as I am hearing myself."

Standing high and lifted up in the pulpit can bestow feelings of importance. Pastors' normal need to experience affirmation from parishioners can be appropriately met through preaching. Painful sensations of being invisible or patronized can also be overcome in those moments when pastors are the center of attention.

At the same time, being high and lifted up leaves pastors highly vulnerable. Preaching exposes their intellectual limitations, their empathic failures, and their spiritual uncertainties. The person of the pastor cannot hide behind the spoken words. While hopefully those words reveal God's work and will in the life-time of parishioners, they inevitably reveal the character of the pastor and the quality of his or her lived-time.

Pastors need to protect their self-cohesion in preaching. Their internal state of being is more important to successful preaching than external sermon style. Many books on how to be a better preacher have little impact on pastors suffering from weakened self-cohesion. Vulnerable pastors come to books on preaching like Pontius Pilate came to the Truth with Jesus. Pilate wanted Jesus to give him Truth, not so that Pilate could be transformed by it, but so that Pilate could own it as a reassuring possession. Similarly, pastors read preaching books for the secure feeling of possessing new knowledge, rather than for opening themselves to needed transformations. Anxieties about not being a good preacher do not usually lead to harder work on sermons, but to shorter work on sermons.

Vacillations in the self-cohesion of pastors result in varied ways of using time in preaching. For example, when pastors enjoy firm self-cohesion, sermon preparation time becomes creative time rather than stewing time. Pastors are better able to "let themselves go" in order to resonate with the deeper meanings of the Scriptures and with the deeper yearnings of parishioners. With firm self-cohesion, time in the pulpit is taken as holy time rather than required time. Self-assured clergy are more willing to risk themselves in front of parishioners, allowing the Holy Spirit to work through them as persons not just as preachers.

When self-cohesion is weak, preparation time either extends beyond appropriate boundaries or is foreshortened. More inclined to feel frustrated with themselves and with parishioners, clergy with damaged self-cohesion use time ineffectually in the pulpit. In spite of their good intentions they tend to afflict the afflicted and comfort the comfortable. Preaching may become a time for ventilation of the pastor's feelings rather than a time for reflective worship. While no book or mentor or counselor can establish appropriate limits or schedules for the amount of time that a particular pastor devotes to preparation for preaching, pastors can assist their own self-cohesion and its effect on their management of time in preaching.

We clergy can protect our self-cohesion and our faithful use of time by trying to stay wise and affirming in our preaching. As we will see, being wise about ourself and parishioners keeps us both creative and balanced in preaching. Affirming ourself and parishioners helps us stay dedicated and encouraging in preaching.

As with pastoral care, we preachers stand in need of God's grace. Our effort to stay wise in our preaching finds grounding in a prayerful attitude expressed by an old hymn: "My gracious Master and my God, assist me to proclaim." Our wisdom alone is insufficient. We are utterly dependent upon God's Spirit to assist us in facing the difficulties of sermon preparation and pulpit delivery.

Beseeching God's assistance also reminds us that the development of our wisdom is not the ultimate goal. As Paul exhorts us, "For we do not proclaim ourselves; we proclaim Jesus Christ as Lord and ourselves as your slaves for Jesus' sake" (2 Cor. 4:5). Our wisdom about ourself and others should serve to make us better witnesses to the presence of Christ in our life-times. Attempts to wisely manage our self and time in preaching must always acknowledge our reliance on God's assistance.

Affirmations of ourself in preaching, and of parishioners in responding, find grounding in the testimony that we are drawn to the divine. God instills within us a yearning for the presence of the Holy. God nurtures in us a longing to feel God near, and to feel an intimate part of God's work in the world. The admonition of another old hymn, which many of us sang growing up, is also a depiction of our heart's desire: "Give of your best to the Master." Our affirmations in preaching are supported by the recognition that however frustrated we might become with ourself or with parishioners, we are all created to seek and respond to God's Word.

BEING WISE ABOUT OURSELF

No preacher ever "arrives." Even seasoned pastors must depend upon God's assistance because they are always struggling to discover what to say and how to say it. But we can endeavor to be wise. In time set aside for sermon preparation, we can wisely face our responses to the creative process, namely the inevitability of creative tensions and the necessity for imagination.

Facing Creative Tensions

Sermon preparation can be intimidating. Like Reverend James, we dread facing the blank page. We dread feeling our stomach tighten as deadlines come closer. We imagine other pastors working serenely in their studies, with ideas flowing smoothly into well-formed words. When we read their wonderfully structured sermons, we chastise ourselves for the jerky, ragtag process we go through when putting a sermon together.

What we need to know, however, is that Reverend James's preparation experiences, and our experiences, are basically normal. There are inevitable tensions that all artists, including preachers, must face in the process of creation.

For example, during creative periods pastors will be exposed to mood swings. These moods will range from precreative depressive feelings to overstimulating joyful feelings. Starting over once again, gearing up for the false starts, and wondering if it is all worthwhile can bring on melancholy. Preaching can sometimes feel as effective as tossing rose petals into the Grand Canyon and waiting for echoes. Expecting absent echoes from parishioners may preface each week's preparation. Apprehension rather than anticipation often marks the beginning of pastors' creativity.

During the process, however, pastors may become excited about a new insight. A rush of pleasure may surge through them, along with thrilling hopes of impressing the congregation. Gooseflesh and hair standing straight may prickle their body. Stomachs may churn with all the excitement. These feelings may be enjoyed but can also be uncomfortable. Pastors may try to shrug them off while still holding on to a warm glow. But even the warm glows tend to fade as further sermon work is required, or as pastors are left flat when rethinking what once seemed so marvelous.

Creativity also involves loneliness. In sermon preparation, pastors not only feel they must carry the burden of preaching alone, they also feel alone when wrestling with a new idea or approach. The task of preaching is a solitary one, and a venture into a different realm of understanding is a lonely one. Normal worries surface as one leaves what is safe. Anxieties about losing one's identity appear as one contemplates changing one's beliefs or perceptions.

Tired bodies, taxed minds, and blows to self-esteem are also part of normal creative tensions. This does not mean that the creative process, and the completed sermon as a created product, cannot be sources of joy for pastors. They most definitely can be. But creative tensions are an integral part of any sermon's preparation.

Creative tensions can threaten self-cohesion. Pastors who lack the ability to regulate internal tensions and bring soothing to themselves are especially vulnerable to creative tensions. Even preachers with firm self-confidence can be intimidated by the stresses of sermon preparation. Firm self-cohesion does not dispel creative tensions. Instead, pastors with firm self-cohesion are able to join with the creative process and to endure its tensions without fragmenting. *When creative tensions are not acknowledged as normal, and as part of the human condition of all pastors, then creative tensions become cohesion threats.* Loneliness then threatens the assurance of belonging. Untested ideas threaten the pastor's hold on reality. Frustrations threaten the ability to cope. Physical demands threaten the pastor's body image. Blankness threatens self-esteem. When creative tensions are not handled wisely, they endanger the self-cohesion of pastors.

When creative tensions are taken as threats to self-cohesion, pastors try to avoid the creative process or to minimize it. In general terms, they become rigid. They use formulas rather than follow the creative process. They try to generate a sermon by purely conscious reason rather than by becoming emotionally involved. They focus more on getting the sermon done than on its pastoral helpfulness. As a result, they fail to use time effectively in sermon preparation.

For example, rather than struggle with the complexities of the Scriptures, the preacher may reduce the meaning of the biblical event to a single principle or truth, thus saying to the congregation, "Today's Scripture tells us . . .". Or rather than trying again and again to understand the particular needs of parishioners, or of the whole congregation, the preacher may offer general prescriptive applications of truth, thus saying, "This applies to our life by . . .". Or rather than wrestle with ways to touch parishioners and alter their habitual thoughts, the preacher may simply exhort them to act differently, thus saying, "Therefore we ought to . . .". Time given to reductive, applicative, or exhortative preaching is essentially wasted. In the long run, this preaching in itself does not touch parishioners' hearts. Attempts to avoid creative tensions often result in rigid sermon methods that fail to illuminate the life-time of parishioners.

Avoidance of creative tensions may also lead pastors to spend too little or too much time in sermon preparation. The former happens, for example, when pastors preach sermons essentially written by others. The latter happens, for example, when pastors dodge concentration. Fearful of facing creative tensions, they avoid concentrating too hard lest they feel inadequate. Consequently they spend much time reading superficially, trying to write before they think, and attempting to fill the spaces between disjointed ideas with watery transitions. They hope something will fall together, but they are apprehensive about owning the sermon process and making it work creatively. Adequate self/time management, however, requires pastors to wisely embrace the normal creative tensions present in sermon preparation.

Employing Imagination

Adequate time management in sermon preparation requires something else besides facing creative tensions. Pastors must also be willing to imagine. Creativity requires an imaginative state that is similar to daydreaming or to child's play. The mental activity of imagination is a free-floating, unfocused attentiveness to whatever comes. It is a readiness to be led rather than to lead, a joyful offer to be captivated by whatever wants to make claims on one's mind.

Imagination grants access. Imagination allows a pastor to visualize what his parishioners are going through, to put himself in their bodies and thus know in his bones how life is for them. With reverent imagination, a pastor hovers attentively over her Scripture lessons and waits for them to speak to her beyond her own expectations. In playful abandonment, clergy allow the collected experiences of their own individual histories to establish resonating links with what they've read and seen. Imagination tries things on for size, permits the clanging together of ideas and feelings that at first seem unrelated, and takes seriously the spontaneous. Reverent imagination is faith-in-the-making, a continual openness to God's divine messages pressing in upon us every day in a thousand different ways.

Firm self-cohesion is the mother of constructive imagination. A reliable sense of consistency and identity allows pastors to give themselves up to the uncertain leadings of imagination. When cohesion is firm, pastors maintain the right priorities in the creative process. The primary mental activity in sermon preparation is made imagination, which is coordinated with and completed by logical thinking and the actual doing of sermon writing.

Imagination does more than facilitate creative use of time in sermon preparation. It is also the shortest and most powerful means for transforming human lives. Parishioners are rarely changed by rational discourse or by ethical admonishments alone. They are changed when their imagination is touched and they feel themselves transported to a different world. The writers of the New Testament knew this. They do not call upon us to be practical but to be poetic, to sense with reverent imagination the meaning of the Incarnation, to preach "not with plausible words of wisdom" but with words of the Spirit that reveal "the mind of Christ" (see 1 Cor. 2). Imaginative reflection is time-efficient in terms of sermon preparation and time-effective in terms of sermon impact.

When the self-cohesion of pastors is weakened, however, the capacity for creative imagination is also weakened. Imagination is belittled or loses its efficacy. Reverend James, for example, was potentially on the right track when he started to open himself to thoughts about the video he had seen. He was letting go, letting the creative process of imaginative play begin its work. Unfortunately he quickly repressed it, declaring it a distraction rather than recognizing it as a prompting of the creative spirit within him.

With the diminution of self-cohesion and imagination, pastors' sermons become sterile. Rather than complementing and completing imagination, reason in sermons may become dominant. Rational discourse about the meaning of the Scriptures, and a reasoned explanation about human needs, may shape the preaching. "He's all head and little heart," declared one parishioner to the church consultant. "We hear about biblical history. We hear about psychology, theology, and politics. But we don't hear a word that makes Monday a little easier to endure."

The doing of sermon writing may also become the dominant activity. Rather than the actual writing of the sermon being a way to order thoughts, or to stimulate further imagination, doing becomes primary. Sermon preparation, for example, may be reduced to supplying content for a perpetual sermon outline. "God's Law," "Man's Disobedience," "Call to Repentance" has been a grooved three-point outline for more than one pastor throughout the decades. All that varied from one Sunday to the next was the supplied content. Other pastors shun imaginative explorations as well as concentrated thinking as they construct skyscraper sermons—one story placed on top of another.

Sermons lacking imaginative input seldom meet parishioners' needs. In that sense they are time deficient. When pastors are led primarily by reverent imagination, coordinated with and completed by the activities of thinking and doing, sermon preparations proceed economically and creatively. While the ability to be imaginative seems inherently stronger in some clergy than others, imagination is a capacity that emerges naturally when self-cohesion is firm. Wise pastors, consequently, do what they can to protect their self-cohesion, and to honor the activity of imagination in the creative process of sermon preparation.

BEING WISE ABOUT OTHERS

Self/time management in preaching requires wisdom about how parishioners deal with change. On the one hand, parishioners profess the need for personal change. They are aware of how their behavior and attitudes hurt others as well as themselves. They look for inspirational guidance that will produce changes in their lives. On the other hand, parishioners yearn for help in dealing with changes that confront them. They realize the necessity of finding ways to cope with new alterations and the attendant anxieties. They look for inspirational guidance that will help them work through the changes in their lives.

Parishioners look for inspirational guidance from their preachers. They seek guidance for how to transform their lives and how to deal with lives that have been transformed. They hope to hear words that will motivate them to change, and words that will help them manage change.

A preacher's responsiveness to these parish expectations may be wedded with the preacher's own pastoral image. By training and experience, the pastor may see himself or herself as both an agent of change and a healer of change. As a result, the preacher may feel specially empowered to serve as parishioners' inspirational guide.

This arrangement, however, must be approached wisely. Blocked efforts to guiding parishioners can threaten the self-cohesion of preachers and their effective use of time. Preachers can maintain their self/time equilibrium by fortifying themselves with two understandings about parishioners: (1) parishioners resist change; and (2) parishioners eventually respond with reduced enthusiasm to the preacher's inspirational guidance.

Acknowledging Resistances to Change

Parishioners resist the pastoral help they request. They both want to change and do not want to change. They expect preachers to move them forward, yet cling to the same spot. They look for clergy to lead them in making social changes, and yet they hold back.

The common reason for resistance to change is stress. All change brings stress. Even joyfully anticipated change disturbs the equilibrium of parishioners, sometimes so much so that the joy is obliterated by the apprehensions. Resistance to change is due not so much to hardness of heart as it is to fright of the soul. Even when detrimental, parishioners hold on tightly to who they feel they are, or to what they think they should do, as if their life depended on it. Emotionally it does.

Change is also slow. Parishioners are not inclined to alter their attitudes or life-styles quickly, although inspired by preaching to do so. Their personalities tend to become set like hardened clay. They, too, need sufficient water and warmth before they can become pliable enough to take new form.

Preachers can preserve their cohesion by wisely responding to parishioners' resistances. For example, insightful pastors do not rely on compliments from parishioners for validation of their preaching effectiveness, or as proof of the power of God in the congregation. They do not readily believe that the compliments received indicate that their preaching has actually penetrated and transformed lives. Such a stance is not cynical. Handshaking parishioners need not be thought of as "the perjury line." Astute preachers are merely realistic. They recognize the difference between social graces and enlightened souls. They discern also the difference between momentary enthusiasm and moved hearts. While preachers can enjoy and even appreciate the good word they hear from parishioners, they ground their self-cohesion on more substantive bases: feeling right with God, feeling authentic and honest, feeling at one with revered preachers past and present.

Wise pastors also recognize the limits of charismatic styled preaching. Fireworks sermons do not usually ignite people into marvelous explosions of new life, except perhaps for short periods of time. Sustained Pentecostal experiences are rare. Pastors maintain their self-cohesion by realizing, instead, that inspirational preaching is more often like keeping a candle lighted in the darkness. It calms fears, warms the heart, and minimizes stumbles as one finds one's way.

Fortified by the understanding that parishioners resist the very changes they desire, pastors manage time adequately. For example, they run the good race of sermon preparation without defeatism. They fight the good fight in the pulpit without bitterness. They own the necessity of providing transformative leadership for the congregation, even when such leadership is unpopular.

Pastors also take a long-term view of preaching. Although welcoming dramatic transformations in parishioners' lives, pastors accept that changes come in slow and mysterious ways through preaching. They manage preparation and pulpit time with the understanding that results are typically delayed if they come at all. "I remember a sermon you preached three years ago, Pastor, when you talked about how God sent Jesus to free us from the fears that keep us from living life abundantly. I was in a bad relationship with a man at the time but couldn't face doing anything about it. Your sermon kept coming back to me.

This week I finally left him." Preachers' time frame for the effectiveness of sermons, therefore, is broad. They think not just in terms of weeks or months, but also in terms of years and lifetimes.

Finally, preachers may dedicate time to being a preparer for change, not just a producer of change. Rather than urge change, they may assume the more indirect role of clearing paths in order for people to make and face changes. Time-sensitive preachers may do this by trying to free individuals from their anxieties about time that impede necessary changes. The litany of those temporality fears is long. "I'm afraid the past will catch up with me." "I can't go back and I can't go forward. The present is all there is, and that's overwhelming." "I'm scared about what will happen in my future." "There's not enough time." "Time is going too fast for me to make a decision." "We're all going to die anyway."

Change forces an anxious awareness of the passing and meaning of one's lived time. Time-resonating preachers realize that making changes and facing changes are closely related to being reconciled to the temporality of life. They strive to help parishioners confront their temporality fears and to own their own lived-time. They remind their congregations that time is God's, and that change is not just an inevitability but the way God works to bring our temporal existence to fruition. Even though adopting a preparer for change stance, pastors must nonetheless wisely acknowledge parishioners' resistances to change.

Embracing Inspirational Decline

Parishioners know there is a difference between the message and the messenger. At times there is a decided emphasis upon wanting to hear the Word rather than wanting to hear the preacher as a person. "Sir, we would see Jesus" was the plaque one church nailed in the pulpit for only the pastor to read.

But the preached word and the preacher are inextricably linked. "I grew up in a small church served by inadequate ministers," said one woman. "I had to try to separate the message from the messenger, but I'm not sure I've ever really been successful at that." Most parishioners are not. Most often they do not even try. The person of the pastor is central in preaching. For better or worse, how parishioners respond to the Word is shaped primarily by how they respond to the preacher as person.

After a certain period, parishioners' increased familiarity with the preacher as a person results in a decrease in their responsiveness to the preacher as their inspirational guide. Familiarity with the person of the preacher reduces the pastor's effectiveness in being able to arouse soul-searching, to enkindle repentance, or to generate moral commitments, on the one hand, or to inspire spiritual feelings, to stimulate hope, or to bring comfort through shared personal experiences, on the other hand. Parishioners may still respond to the preacher's teaching in the pulpit, or to directions for church life, but the power to shape how parishioners deal with changes in their lives declines.

Increased familiarity leads to a wide range of reduced responses to the inspirational guidance of the preacher. At one end, parishioners *reject* the preacher's guidance when they judge the pastor's behavior as incompetent or reprehensible. Parishioners tend to *minimize* the preacher's guidance when over time they become personally disappointed in how the pastor has acted in committees or in pastoral care situations, or when they have been related to basically in a "buddy buddy" way by the pastor. Parishioners' responses become *diminished* when they simply know the preacher too well. "When he gets up in the pulpit, he's just my husband talking," said one wife of a pastor. Parishioners' increased familiarity with the preacher results in this same kind of "emperor with his clothes off " attitude. Over time, familiarity results in a natural attrition of the preacher's inspirational influence.

Finally, at the other end, parishioners become *desensitized* to even the most consistently inspiring preachers. Stimulus saturation sets in. Just as an inspiring mountain scene loses its luster when one drives by it day after day, the inspirational efforts of the preacher lose their impact when parishioners hear the preacher year after year.

Familiarity dissipates specialness. The inspirational role preachers have in shaping how parishioners confront change declines as familiarity develops. As a result, the self-cohesion of preachers is threatened. Even pastors with firm self-cohesion experience a sense of being devalued. The greater the decline in influence and/or the more innately vulnerable the self of the preacher, the more extensive the damage to the preacher's self-cohesion.

Pastors' belief that they have matured as a preacher may be shaken when their religious urgings are responded to with less enthusiasm. Clergy may begin to doubt themselves when their guidance seems to fall on deaf ears. Despair may set in when they realize that their history of committed efforts for the church will not ensure their role as revered inspirational leaders. Questions about whether they are burned out or should leave the ministry may also surface disturbingly.

Pastors are likewise pained when they do not feel accepted for who they are. They long to be able to be their real self, in the pulpit and out, and still be turned to for moral leadership and pastoral solace. The issue of familiarity, therefore, may make them anxious about personal sharing in sermons. They may become apprehensive about crossing that indefinite line between self-revelations that are appreciated by parishioners, and those that parishioners take as disappointing.

Weakened self-cohesion shapes how clergy use time in preaching. Pastors upset by the impact of familiarity may reduce time spent in sermon preparation and delivery. "I preach shorter and shorter sermons, not because I'm better at it but because it seems a waste of time. People still want me to visit the sick and keep the church's programs running, but they don't seem moved by my preaching anymore. So, I put my time elsewhere."

Quality of time may also suffer. The gospel message may be delivered flatly, in a take-it-or-leave-it style, with preachers deliberately screening from their sermons any personal references. Hurt by what they interpret as a "what have you done for me today" attitude on the part of parishioners, some preachers stop trying to provide inspirational guidance at all. Little direction is given for moral renewal, or for becoming a change agent in society. Only perfunctory suggestions are made for facing life anew when change destroys the customary.

Frustrated clergy may also use pulpit time as enforcement time. Feeling righteously indignant that the transforming message of Jesus is made dependent upon the familiar vessel that proclaims it, pastors may adopt a relentlessly prophetic stance in the pulpit. This approach masks an underlying rage of pastors who covertly declare: "You may not take me seriously anymore, but by God you'd better take God's Word seriously! Woe to you unless you do!" The shepherd who cannot lead becomes one who drives.

Wise pastors understand the effects of familiarity. Familiarity does not necessarily breed contempt, but it does reduce responses to the preacher's role as inspirational guide.

Wise preachers, however, can wrestle a blessing from familiarity. They can preserve their self-cohesion in the face of this loss by embracing it as a humbling experience. For example, some clergy, young and old, enter the pulpit with inflated egos. They feel a power surging through their words and actions that they think will change those they meet. They secretly believe that the magnetism of their presence in the pulpit will inspire parishioners to new life.

Familiarity dispels grandiosity. This experience may be devastating for a time, but it can lead preachers to reaffirm that it is ultimately God's Spirit and not theirs that brings healing changes, and brings healing to changes. While they can recognize the importance of the preacher as person, they can focus on being a person of integrity and faithfulness rather than playing the role of acclaimed guide. They can continue to reach their potential for inspiration because the message inspires them and because they are called upon to do their best.

Embracing familiarity can also increase the capacity for sensing parishioners' time. When the progressive flow of a parishioner's history is disturbed, the self-cohesion of that parishioner is also disturbed. Job demotions, layoffs, or forced retirements disturb one's anticipated timing. Time is out of synch. Events happen before their expected arrival. The internal clock that parishioners have inside them, which informs them when certain events should normally occur, and when they will be ready to adjust to them, suddenly no longer applies. They are forced to adjust their internal timetable, and with it the overall story of their life.

Pastors know firsthand what it means to eventually lose the anticipated unfolding of one's lived-time. They realize how abilities that once were expected to grant a person continuous importance gradually fade with time. Empathy for parishioners' lived-time increases when preachers themselves experience how the present loses the comfort of the past, when cherished self-images are devalued.

Finally, accepting familiarity can also enhance the capacity for revealing time. Reduction of power points to the temporality of all life. Nothing lasts forever. The preacher acknowledges his or her finitude represented by the dwindling of influence and position.

Such boundary experiences can reinstate a dependence upon God. The preacher's newly shaped humility, in the pulpit and out, becomes a quiet witness to our daily reliance on God's care. Sermon time, therefore, may become even more an occasion of thanks for all God has done, is doing, and will do in our lifetime.

AFFIRMING OURSELF

Walter Burghardt once made this assessment: "The effectiveness of my preaching often seems directly proportionate to the agony of mind, spirit, and flesh I endure."[1] Many of us could take that as an indictment of our preaching. We try to slide by unperturbed. Others of us will groan aloud if Burghardt's personal assessment applies generally. We cringe at the prospect of needing to suffer for preaching's sake.

Although this assessment cannot be universalized—effective preaching can emerge from lightness of spirit, and agonized preparations can lead to beautiful moments but awful sermon hours—it does prompt recognition of what preachers should affirm. *The pain they endure is holy.* The sacrifices of mind, spirit, and flesh in preaching are borne sufferings, carried for the sake of the gospel and the redemption of others. Creative tensions, nauseating anxiety when entering the pulpit, post-sermon blues, and weariness of spirit when preparations must begin again are precious offerings of the preacher's very self to the ministry of the Word.

The preacher may not feel so nobly dedicated. The agonies of sermon preparation and delivery may be despised. For the preacher they may represent intellectual or spiritual weakness. They may be taken as occupational hazards, or be responded to as sufferings the victimized pastor must endure.

Pains in preaching need to be redeemed. They are more than part of the job. In the best sense they are offered sacrifices. They are expenditures of the preacher's own self and own lived-time, never to be reclaimed. Pieces of the preacher are lost, no matter how beneficial those sacrifices might be. Those sacrifices may be grieved over at times. They should always be honored.

Endured pains are honorable no matter what the condition of the preacher. The sermon struggles of a fragile pastor are as laudable as those of a self-assured one. The endured pains are honorable no matter what the quality striven for. Efforts to simply put a sermon together are as commendable as efforts to find a right word or illustration. The endured pains are honorable no matter what the size of the congregation. Agonizing over what to say to thirty parishioners is as meritorious as agonizing over what to say to three thousand. Appreciation for pastors is increased when both pastors and parishioners consecrate preachers' pain as offered sacrifices.

When preachers affirm themselves in this way, they contribute to the firmness of their own self-cohesion. They confront disquieting experiences and take them into their self. Painful experiences that once seemed "not me" or "destroying me" are now embraced as "part of me." Creative tensions become "part of my creative nature." Dismay over the time spent in preparation becomes "part of my call to give my best." Anxieties about preaching become "part of my desire to lift people out of their routine existence." Trepidations about exposing oneself become "part of my willingness to be foolish for the gospel's sake." The self of the preacher expands to include that which once felt meaningless or overwhelming. Self-cohesion matures as pastors allow their selves to embrace more of their life-time experiences. That can happen in part when preachers affirm the consecrated nature of their sacrifices.

Affirming the sacrificial nature of preaching efforts can aid pastors in using time effectively. While pastors will need periodically to reaffirm the meaning of their preaching struggles as a way of maintaining self-cohesion, this affirmation can become a background support that preachers need not rub constantly for reassurance. On an economic level, therefore, they are free to get on with the work of preaching rather than having to work to free themselves for preaching. Cohesion is present rather than solicited. More time can be given to the task instead of to emotional preparation for the task.

Furthermore, preachers' strengthened self-cohesion

via affirming themselves minimizes the need to spend time in regressive attempts to maintain self-cohesion. Self-pity over preaching struggles will not be wallowed in as a means for soothing preachers' creative tensions, and time in self-aggrandizement will not be needed as a way of sustaining self-cohesion in the face of familiarity's impact. Finally, firmly cohered pastors will not comfort themselves with the idea that their sacrifices excuse giving less than their best. Sermon sacrifices do not condone haphazard efforts. Instead, the life-time pastors give to preaching is made "a fragrant offering, a sacrifice acceptable and pleasing to God" (Phil. 4:18). Self-affirmation leads to giving one's best to the Master.

AFFIRMING OTHERS

According to the National Institute of Mental Health, anxiety constitutes the most prevalent mental health problem in the United States. If preachers take time to look up from their manuscripts, they will see pews filled with anxious individuals. If they take a clue from what they see, many preachers will look down again and alter their manuscripts.

Pride is a sermon staple. Theology is replete with analysis of pride as the root of sin, or the equivalent of sin. The aim of much Christian preaching and biblical exegesis is to produce "conviction of sin" by convincing persons that they think too highly of themselves.

There is justification in calling people to account when their self-glorification estranges them from God, their neighbors, and their best self. But perhaps the last thing the preacher needs to warn people about is their pride. The pews are not filled with individuals puffed up with pride. They are filled with souls bereft of pride. Those who come to hear God's word are harder on themselves than anyone else. There are many parishioners who are smart, amazing, and doing things of great courage who do not believe in themselves. They lead anxious lives rather than arrogant lives. To inveigh against pride in sermons is to be neither pastorally observant nor psychologically astute. It contributes neither to firm self-cohesion nor to faithful use of time.

Preachers need to affirm parishioners' pride. A person's pride is a God-given satisfaction. It is a natural experience when a person enjoys firm self-cohesion. At the same time pride enhances a person's self-cohesion. One becomes one's best self under the warming sun of another's praise. No doubt Jesus carried on his ministry heartened by God's words of affirmation: "This is my Son, the Beloved, with whom I am well pleased" (Matt. 3:17).

Healthy pride is also the most fruitful condition for the springing forth of love. Just as for pastors, people are more apt to be caring when their self-cohesion is firm. Preaching that affirms the goodness of parishioners' pride is time-effective in terms of both restoring well-being and increasing empathy for others. Conversely, the self-cohesion of parishioners is injured, and time is nonproductive, when pride as sin is made central in preaching.

Finally, is the self-cohesion of preachers made firmer when they are motivated by a vision of people as tragic souls suffering from lost pride or by a vision of people as guilty sinners manifesting arrogant pride? Although pastors might stress the truth in both visions, a case could be made for the former. Preachers manifest greater empathy and compassion for others—signs of firm self-cohesion—

when they view people as struggling to hold themselves together but inevitably falling apart and falling short of their created goodness. Preachers' self-cohesion is also fortified when they affirm that we live in the glow of a God who encourages more than condemns.

Chapter Five

Self/Time Management

in Church Administration

Reverend Marten sat in the church council meeting trying to remember her role. I'm a pastor first and an administrator second, she thought. No, I'm a pastor in *all* situations, including administration. What is most important are the human relationships in each meeting I'm in. My calling is to bring people closer together and closer to God. If I can do that, then people will respond with cooperative and thankful hearts.

Her own heart, however, felt as it had with the late night caller: irritated. The council was limping along in its old unproductive ways. Her directions for improvements had been listened to but politely reasoned away, as they too often were as far as she was concerned.

A line from a seminary professor came to mind. "Let the preferences of the untutored many be superior over the planning of the expert few." She had struggled with that then, and was struggling with it now. She felt absolutely sure of what should be done, and it certainly wasn't what the untutored many had in mind. What kind of leadership was best? When was struggling for control a necessity for the life of the congregation and when was it counterproductive? Was she Pollyannaish to think that bringing people closer to one another and to God would make them more unified and considerate?

Waking up from her ruminating, she surprised herself, and the council, by suddenly standing up and blurting assertively, "I have had years of experience in this area, and I know what I'm talking about. You called me to be your minister, and that means giving direction to the church. What you're planning hasn't worked and won't work. You need to listen to what I'm telling you." Instantly she wondered if she had gone too far. Still inflamed by her emotions, she looked them in the eye and waited for a response.

SELF-COHESION AND CHURCH ADMINISTRATION

Pastors in church administration seldom enjoy what Mark Twain called "the calm confidence of a Christian holding four aces." More than any other dimension of ministry today, church administration is an interactive venture between clergy and laity. In the past, the balance of influence between pastor and laity typically favored the former. Furthermore, people were chosen to boards in the church not because of their executive qualities but because they possessed the character that gave dignity to the office.

Organizational models that encourage shared administrative leadership are now being increasingly adopted by churches and denominations across the country. Church constitutions and bylaws are being revised to access the broadest involvement of parishioners in the guidance of church life. People are elected to church boards based on their expertise in areas of management and finances developed in their employment fields.

Shared leadership with parishioners can be relieving for pastors. There is comfort in knowing one does not have to go it alone. At the same time, shared leadership can heighten pastors' tensions. Parishioners are not the untutored many, but experts who can and do challenge what is being done, including suggestions by clergy leaders. Pastors are forced to rethink their leadership role, and to wrestle with how much persuasion to use in various instances. They can no longer rely on their role to give them credence, but must demonstrate wise administrative insights. In addition, pastors are also expected to ease group tensions and maintain an overall religious perspective for the work being done.

In this administrative enterprise with laity, it is hoped that ministers learn to "play the cards dealt them," as an old denominational leader used to say. That means not only having a pastoral strategy but also possessing the self-cohesion necessary to deal with the heightened tensions of administrative work.

Clergy inevitably experience injuries in church administration. Like Reverend Marten, even the most self-confident pastors are prone to anger when they feel treated as auxiliary items, for example. Their anger may produce needed results. It may be justified. It may even create a new image of the pastor as strong. But pastors' chests often stay tight after such eruptions. Leadership by outburst is rarely reassuring. Pastors suffer a double blow: the threat to their self when their leadership efforts are thwarted, and the blow to their own self-esteem for having lost emotional control, especially in front of others.

Withdrawal rather than anger may be the response when pastors feel that their leadership is criticized. One clergyman was berated by certain members of his council for not taking matters into his own hands and making important decisions they deemed necessary. The barrage left him shaken. Although he continued to participate in council meetings, he did so with diminished enthusiasm. A more severe withdrawal reaction would have been to become more of an observer at council meetings than a participant. An even more severe reaction would have been to absent himself frequently from council meetings.

The state of the pastor's self-cohesion determines the effectiveness of the pastor's administrative leadership. More specifically, it shapes the pastor's use of time. On a personal level, for example, pastors with damaged self-cohesion may spend church time licking wounds, eliciting support if not sympathy from parishioners, or simply trying to get even. On a professional level, pastors with weakened self-cohesion may consume time by constantly restructuring administrative procedures, by dealing with every disruption in the church as an administrative problem, or by striving to impose administrative changes on the congregation.

The state of the pastor's self-cohesion also influences the effectiveness of laity's leadership. In general, a calm pastor generates confidence. An inspiring pastor arouses zeal. An anxious pastor breeds agitation. A belligerent pastor stimulates mistrust. A disinterested pastor produces listlessness. No matter how much leadership laity assume, they are affected by the state of the pastor's self. Parishioners' sensitivities to the mood of their pastor are not diminished by changing organizational formats (from "pastor-centered" to "parish-centered," for example), or by changing what the pastor's role is called (from "pastoral office" to "pastoral function," for example), or by changing what the pastor is expected to do (from "guiding" laity to "resourcing" laity, for example). Disruptions in the self of the pastor, no matter how or where they originate, create disruptions in the cohesion of the congregation. More specifically, they create disturbances in the cohesion of lay leaders, and thus disturbances of their effective use of time in administrative efforts.

In short, maintenance of the pastor's own self-cohesion is a professional necessity in church administration. By adequately managing self and time, pastors short-circuit the emotional reactions that would otherwise pump them full of adrenaline and tell them to fight or flee. When managing self and time adequately, pastors position themselves to lead effectively, and to enable lay leaders to minister as productively as they can.

As in other areas of ministry, clergy can foster their own self-cohesion, and respond well to the time needs of parishioners through administrative work, by acting wisely and affirmingly. On the one hand, pastors can wisely monitor their own timing in administration and steadfastly avoid executivism. They can also recognize time arrow and time cycle needs/demands of congregations and respond appropriately. On the other hand, pastors can foster adequate self/time management by affirming the importance of their attentiveness to mundane administrative tasks, and by affirming trust in laity.

When the quarreling disciples asked Jesus which one among them would become the greatest, Jesus gave a response that can spiritually guide our attempts to be wise and affirming in our administrative work: "Truly I tell you, unless you change and become like children, you will never enter the kingdom of heaven" (Matt. 18:3).

To be wise about ourself and parishioners in church administration requires the willingness to let ourself engage the world with the primordial sensitivities God gave us as children. As children we took at face value what we experienced and what others promised us. We knew through our nerve endings when people were hurting. In direct and innocent ways we expressed our own needs and exposed the actions of others. In spite of Paul's assertive announcement that he had matured and "put an end to childish ways" (1 Cor. 13:11), Jesus reminds us of the importance of remaining childlike in our understanding. These are gifts of knowing to be enhanced by our maturing reason, not condemned as something to outgrow. In church administration, being wise as a serpent helps us maintain a constant vigilance against negative forces. That is not enough. We also need wisdom born of childish innocence that helps us resonate with essential things no eye can see.

Affirmations of ourself and laity in church administration may be sustained by understanding that all of us are but children coming to Jesus. For all our sophistication, we are just hungry, hurting children of God, crowding around the feet of Jesus, looking for reassurance and love. Clergy and lay leaders' goal of establishing the Kingdom should never take precedence over the affirmation that we are but children who yearn for the King. Our affirmations in themselves are not holy unless they spring from a wider embrace of people as children of God.

BEING WISE ABOUT OURSELF

Living one's time and being dedicated to the task of administration are admirable traits. When not wisely checked, however, they can lead to damaged self-cohesion and ineffective use of time. Pastors maintain healthy management of self and time in administrative work by monitoring their timing and by avoiding executivism.

Monitoring Our Timing

"I'm a stormer," said one pastor. "I tend to lay back on projects until near the deadline and then I storm to get the task accomplished." "I move slowly through one project at a time," stated another. "I become absorbed in finishing one task before I begin the next one." "I like things rapid fire," added a third. "I like to see that big pile of stuff go down, down, down. When things aren't popping, I get restless."

Each pastor has an internal time clock that paces her or his action. Each one's clock is set differently, with some running faster and others slower. For every event, and for life in general, each pastor tends to operate according to the timing that seems normal to him or her. When the timing of events exceeds the pastor's own internal time, the pastor becomes uncomfortable and tries to speed events up or slow them down until they more nearly match the pastor's own timing pattern.

A pastor's internal time clock shapes the timing of administrative work. At the very least, a pastor expects that personal timing habits will be tolerated by the congregation. "I work at my own pace. That should not be the congregation's worry as long as I get the job done." More often, however, clergy expect that the congregation will mold itself to the pastor's own timing preferences. "Council business should move swiftly. There's no need for long deliberations before decisions are made. I like to get things in and over with."

The self-cohesion of pastors is strengthened when they

experience others accepting them and being like them. The assured feeling that others share their goals and even their sense of timing in doing things contributes to pastors' internal sense of well-being.

But when parishioners are critical of the pastor's time habits, or resist an administrative style for the whole church based on the pastor's sense of timing, then the cohesion of the pastor is threatened. Depending upon the prior vulnerability of the pastor's self, he or she responds with varying degrees of anger or withdrawal. A pastor infuriated because lay leaders were not attending the accelerated number of council meetings the pastor had instituted, retained parishioners in church on Sundays by preaching hour-long sermons. Another pastor said: "I hear complaints indirectly that I move too slow, not just in talking to people or trying to get things done but even in how I pace Sunday morning worship. What I'm trying to do is be deliberate, thoughtful. It gets me down to think they don't realize this."

When self-cohesion is weakened, effective use of time is jeopardized even more. For example, injured pastors may exhibit the Hamlet syndrome. "Time," lamented Hamlet, "is out of joint," and it remained for him alone "to set it right" (Act I, scene 5). Fragmenting pastors may adopt this same desperate approach with congregations. They may declare that the church is "behind time," or "running out of time," and thus take it as their administrative duty "to set it right." They take their own time as the right time, as the proper assessment of what is necessary, and they demand that the congregation accommodate to their timetables and time patterns. These pastors engage in a wide variety of tactics to force congregational compliance: silent treatments, angry outbursts, secret alliances, or threats to resign and start another church, for example. They take the setting right of time as a personal responsibility, which they feel entitled, if not empowered, to make a reality.

Like Hamlet, however, they fail to realize how their need to set time right springs from their own fragmentation. Hamlet was driven to right time because his own lived time, his own self-cohesion, was out of joint. In order to ease his internal pain and regain a sense of sanity, he tried to reshape the world's time, to make it accommodate to his sense of what was proper. Time-righting became a crusade championed basically by his fragmentation. The same happens with some pastors who have lost their self-cohesion.

Wise pastors monitor their tendency to bend administration to their own personal timing. They realize the threats to their self-cohesion when the church is critical of their use of time, or when the church's time is out of joint with theirs. They do what they can to expand their tolerance of timings different than their own without losing their own identity or sense of leadership. They also search for opportunities, in the church and out, where they can give free expression to their own unique timing needs.

At all times, however, they remember that the church's time and their time is but lent to them by God. We are all, in the truest sense, living on borrowed time. Humble acknowledgment of this keeps us centered.

Avoiding Executivism

In 1926 William H. Leach wrote an insightful book entitled *Church Administration: A Survey of Modern Executive Methods.* He noted that the development of the administrative side of the pastor's work was relatively new. He strongly suggested that it may be "part of truth and wisdom, however, to treat this phase of activity not as a separate and new thing, but only as a broader interpretation of pastoral service." He then made the prediction that the installation of administrative work, especially work centered around finances, "will lead . . . to a new conception of a minister's duties."[1]

Leach's prediction was highly accurate. It is now common to conceptualize the role of the pastor as that of an administrative executive, whose paid duty is to work with lay volunteers in managing the business of the church.

Leach's suggestion, however, has not prevailed. For some clergy, administrative work has not only superseded the interpretation that it is just part of pastoral service, it has also become its own interpreter—and advocate. Administration now self-justifies itself. It is a practice with its own terminology and techniques, with its own journals and workshops.

But more than that, for some pastors administrative work has become *the primary interpreter* by which other aspects of ministry are viewed. Pastoral activities like preaching, teaching, and visitation are treated as means for keeping the church operative. Concerns for church growth and institutional maintenance shape pastoral decisions. Programs and activities become part of the "broader interpretation" of "running the church." Leach's suggestion is turned on its head, and with it much of ministry that has stressed the primacy of relationships over administrative functioning.

Wise pastors realize that self-cohesion is jeopardized when clergy function primarily as executive managers rather than relating pastors. In the first place, even though administrative leadership may receive public validation in seminaries or congregations, pastors sense a betrayal of their calling when they place functions before people. Most pastors who report God calling them into ministry speak of feeling called to care. When doing things is placed before nurturing relationships, pastors feel unfaithful, and ultimately unfulfilled. "I've tried to push the uneasiness away, or attribute it to overwork," said one pastor. "When I finally let myself be honest with myself, I realized how much I had changed. I had veered from my values more than I ever realized. That was scary, to know I could be that far off-track without realizing it. But it also made me cry like a child who wanted to get back into a good relationship with a loving parent. I know it doesn't sound very sophisticated, but I feel better now holding God's hand."

When integrity is lost, so, then, is self-cohesion. Recognizing that we are off-track by being too functionally oriented is often like recognizing we are sick. We feel bad long before we admit we have any symptoms, and long before we are willing to take our medicine. Wise clergy recognize the signs as well as the cause of this depletion of the pastor's self and make the necessary changes.

In the second place, congregational need also threatens the self-cohesion of pastors who adopt an executive approach. Although administrative ability may be a high priority when parishioners select a pastor, and while a well-run church is a delight to the congregation, when parishioners are hurting, the administrative competency of the pastor is of little importance. When parishioners lie in a hospital bed or stand beside the open grave of a loved one, they are not impressed with how well the pastor can manage stewardship drives. They want, instead, a pastor who can give a look and say a word that soothes their fear. They want a pastor with a graceful presence who can help them live fully the time of their life, even its most difficult moments. They yearn for a hopeful vision of God working caringly in their allotted time.

Executive-oriented pastors might be able to do this, but their responses tend to be practiced rather than natural and genuine. More to the point, pastors court disaster when they assume that parishioners primarily expect administrative management from their clergy. "I was called to give this church strong leadership, but now I'm accused of being cold and calculating," said one pastor after six months in a new parish. "There's not one word of complaint about administrative decisions I've implemented, just people saying that they don't feel comfortable with me. One group in the church has even complained to our denomination. I really don't understand what they're upset about. There is nothing concrete that I've done wrong! I'm just about ready to explode."

A parishioner's elemental need is for caring pastors. A pastor overly invested in administration, therefore, stands vulnerable to criticism—if not dismissal. Complaints about pastoral leadership are rarely about organizational matters themselves. They are principally about feeling disappointed in the person of the pastor. A clear mandate to provide administrative leadership does not protect a pastor from a parishioner's unspoken yearning for the comfort of the pastor's personal self, and a well-functioning church is not a safeguard against parishioners' eventual disillusionment with administrative-minded clergy.

Even when the self-cohesion of pastors is not disrupted, their executive-dominated approaches utilize time in nonrelational ways. Time is dealt with as "production time," that is, time as measured and assessed in light of the accomplishment of goals and objectives. Time is less likely to be treated as "process time," that is, time as measured and considered in terms of the process of human interactions going on in the achieving of goals, where the lives of individuals in administration are more important than the administration itself.

When the self-cohesion of pastors is fragmented, time management becomes even more ineffective. Like all pastors when their equilibrium is disturbed, administrative-minded pastors' capacity for considering alternative approaches is weakened. In an effort to regain feelings of security, they hold on ever more tenaciously to their customary ways. More specifically, when faced with personal or congregational disruptions, they intensify their administrative efforts.

For example, clergy may spend considerable time trying to refine their administrative approach. They may urge lay leaders to work harder, or may add a new committee, or may urge a revision of administrative procedures. Clergy may take time management courses in order to increase their efficiency, or they may set up a time management workshop in the church for lay leaders.

In addition, complaints in the church may be ignored or minimized as clergy interpret these as administrative problems rather than relationship problems. "The real difficulty comes from some of the financial decisions that the former pastor made. When we clear them up, people will be happy again."

If relationship difficulties persist, and are finally acknowledged, the very administrative approaches contributing to the difficulties may be used as the solutions. One pastor devised a "task force" to uncover and analyze parishioners' complaints of feeling manipulated. Another pastor, who was accused of being more interested in church management than being with people, suggested that an associate be hired who could take care of "the interpersonal side of the congregation."

Solutions by administration seldom work. They not only waste time, they also fail to address the personal life-time needs of parishioners. Administrative solutions dwell on getting people to do what they are expected to do, not on what is personally meaningful in the process. An overly administrative focus, furthermore, tends to lump individuals into a collective understanding, in which clergy lose the sense of ministering to individuals as they address themselves to the congregation as a corporate whole.

The more severe the loss of self-cohesion, the more intense may become clergy's time commitment to administration as a means for personal and parish restoration. When the attendance of one church began to drop steadily, the frightened pastor pushed for tightening of the budget and for hiring an outside firm to audit the books. When intense mistrust arose between a senior pastor and the church staff, the highly threatened senior demanded that each staff member keep an hourly record of their work and monthly present it to the personnel committee.

Franz Kafka's character, Gregor Samsa, wakes up one morning to find himself transformed into a gigantic insect. But rather than agonize over the meaning of his metamorphosis, he worries about how he is going to make it to work on time.[2] Pastors, like Samsa, can become inappropriately preoccupied with administrative details at those very moments when their lives and the congregation's are undergoing massive transformations. When this happens, time for administration rather than time for soul searching becomes more than denial; it becomes a tragedy.

Wise clergy come to realize that one of the highest forms of self-deceit is to believe that a primary commitment of time to administrative functions will ultimately serve the relational needs of parishioners. Not only do congregations then suffer but so also do pastors themselves. Pastors preserve their own self-cohesion and effective use of time when they guard against administrative excesses.

BEING WISE ABOUT OTHERS

Congregations, like pastors, have their own temporal expectations. On the one hand, they expect to move forward. Parishioners attend and support the church assuming that the church's life has direction and purpose, that it is going somewhere. We can call this the church's "time arrow" expectation.

On the other hand, congregations expect consistency. Parishioners come to church assuming that the church's life will be constant, that it will have an abiding sameness week after week that they can rely on. We can call this the church's "time cycle" expectation.

Time arrow and time cycle expectations operate implicitly within congregations. They are taken for granted as something that naturally does and should happen. As long as these expectations are adequately met, congregations experience a sense of well-being. They feel enlivened by the thought of having direction, that they are progressing. They feel comforted by the thought of having continuity, that they are permanent.

Pastors are designated timekeepers. Congregations rely

upon their clergy to maintain a temporal order that guarantees both advance and sameness. Administration is a key means by which clergy are expected to preserve congregational cohesion by fulfilling time arrow and time cycle expectations.

When the cohesion of a congregation weakens, its temporal needs intensify. The congregation becomes more conscious, and anxious, about reestablishing a sense that its lived time has direction and/or continuity.

Time arrow needs, on the one hand, intensify according to the level of the congregation's fragmentation. For example, if a congregation suffers minor fragmentation, it may urge its clergy to make administrative decisions that will move the church toward "fulfillment of its avowed course." Shaken by some injury to itself, the congregation yearns to experience itself moving definitely toward an enhanced state, where, in spite of its trouble, it is getting better and better.

If the congregation suffers moderate fragmentation, it may simply urge clergy to make administrative decisions that "set things on the right course again." Increased anxiety leads to requests for reestablishing the former status quo. Moving toward fulfillment of its direction becomes less important to the congregation at this point than being assured that it *is* moving in a direction.

When fragmentation is severe, the congregation may urge its clergy to "set a course." Having lost its center, the congregation may rely upon administrative interventions from the pastor to assure the congregation that it even *has* a direction.

Time cycle needs, on the other hand, also intensify in proportion to damaged self-cohesion. For example, congregations suffering minor fragmentation may urge administrative decisions that "lift up and honor" those activities, experiences, or symbols that gave the congregation its secure identity through the years.

When fragmentation is moderate, congregations may press the pastor to make administrative decisions that "restore" familiar and customary ways. The congregation feels that more than honoring tradition is needed at this point. Reinstatement of past acts and rituals is called for by the congregation as a means for regaining self-cohesion.

If fragmentation is severe, congregations may demand administrative decisions from clergy that "create" a sense of continuity that the congregation lacks.

Meeting the congregation's time arrow and time cycle expectations is normally an administrative challenge. When a congregation suffers fragmentation, its administrative demands may be experienced as a threat. The self-cohesion of pastors stands on the line.

Pastors may feel professionally threatened by the difficulty of calmly instituting an administrative plan. To some degree, vulnerable churches tend either to become self-protective and resistant to change (attempts to regain comforting feelings of continuity) or to flee into new, untried ventures (attempts to regain comforting feelings of having direction). The more severely fragmented the congregation the less tolerance it has for enduring difficulties or for long-range planning. Solutions are wanted quickly. When a pastor is not able to swiftly heal the hemorrhaging of a congregation's cohesion, the pastor is likely to be seen as an ineffective administrator.

Pastors may also feel personally threatened. Congregations whose self-cohesion is fragmenting lose their full capacity for empathy. They can become desperate, and in their effort to regain equilibrium can easily treat the pastor more as a hired employee than a professional. Pastors working with troubled churches often feel not only pressured, but lonely, and personally devalued.

When self-cohesion is weakened, a pastor uses administrative time in less effective ways. Feeling pressured to perform, a pastor may launch impulsively into some administrative solution without reflecting on the time needs of the congregation. For example, a church riddled with controversy may need administration that meets needs for assured continuity and consistency (time cycle needs). The pastor, however, may initiate steps that focus on directionality (time arrow efforts). The pastor may energetically attempt to get the church to open itself to new changes when the church's need is to hold on rather than move on.

Or the opposite may occur. The church may need assurance of directionality while the pastor may work to maximize consistency. The church feels the need for life-imbuing movement, while the pastor attempts to slow the church down and consolidate itself.

Time may also be used ineffectively when pastors get caught up in solutions by suspicion. Pressured to find solutions, pastors may begin to suspect that specific other churches have found the secrets for success, and so they commit considerable time trying to uncover those secrets. Or pastors may suspect that churches in general are on the right track, and so they take the common average of what churches in general are doing as the solution for their particular congregation's problem. Not infrequently, however, other pastors are doing the same, and so changes that come are made not on substance but on suspicion. Administrative adjustments are reached more through alchemy than by assessment of the congregation's time needs.

Being wise about the time expectations of congregations, and about the expression of these expectations when congregations become fragmented, helps pastors preserve their self-cohesion and competent use of time. What also helps is wisely realizing the limits of one's experience.

Pastors' administrative experience dealing with minor crises in the church does not prepare them for dealing with major crises in the church. Thankfully there is some transfer of knowledge from the former to the latter, but the assumption that "all crises in churches are basically alike," or that years of experience in one church will equip a pastor to deal with all problems in another church, is erroneous. Churches with historically unstable cohesion create effects that are more frequent, more sudden, and more profound in their impact than those found in basically stable churches with typical crises, or in stable churches with momentarily severe crises. Clergy who know how to deal with ground fire crises are not automatically prepared to deal with the distinctively different forces of forest fire crises.

Pastors protect their self-cohesion, therefore, by soliciting help when in crisis situations that are unfamiliar to them. They can ask denominational officials to consult with them about their administrative efforts. At times they can request direct assistance at the church. They can seek training in crisis management, and can learn from other seasoned pastors. Such solicitations are not signs of weakness on pastors' part but signs of wisdom. Prompted by vestiges of our childhood wisdom, we turn naturally to others for help when facing the strange and overwhelming.

AFFIRMING OURSELF

It has been estimated that leaders contribute on the average no more than 20 percent to the success of most organizations.[3] That statistic might apply to secular leadership, but it certainly does not seem descriptive of pastors' contributions. Leaders in secular organizations are likely to adopt a popular management style known as "Management by Wandering About." Here the leader is skilled at delegating and staying out of the way. His or her central task is to wander among the workers wherever they may be, motivating them and creating a relaxed environment for them so they can do their best and be most productive. Noninterference is practiced except when absolutely necessary. With an approach like this, perhaps the leader does contribute only 20 percent in terms of actual administrative input.

But can you imagine a "Ministry by Wandering About" style? There will be elements of this approach in pastors' work, but in reality most administration is "Ministry by Getting One's Fingernails Dirty." That means simply that pastors become involved in the hard, often tedious, frontline work of keeping the church organized. Big pillar administrative decisions are rare. Most of church life depends upon faithful attentiveness to mundane administrative tasks. Without such attentiveness, however, the church would falter.

This attentiveness is not glamorous. Anyone who listens to the bulk of a pastor's administrative conversation will basically hear the pastor trying to arrange for a babysitter so parents can attend a church meeting, or discussing how many tables need to be set up for a church dinner, or thinking through with others whether the men's restroom should be repainted by a local painter in the church or by the senior high youth group as their service project.

Routine administrative tasks are often difficult as well. Pastors wrestle with how to pay for roof repairs, when to contact individuals who have not met their pledge, or what to do with a teacher who uses class time to express biased religious views. Charles de Gaulle once observed that a country with 246 cheeses could not be governed. Pastors often feel the same about congregations who have 246 different opinions about every decision. Administration requires the ability to endure not only the lack of public acclaim but also the pinches that come with serving.

Pastors' attentiveness to mundane administrative tasks is praiseworthy. It is an honorable service, hardly ever appreciated with clear understanding by laity, and often minimized by clergy themselves. Pastors, however, can, and should, affirm themselves for their willingness to immerse themselves in the nitty-gritty of daily administration. Their efforts are the common mortar that hold the church together.

More significantly, if God is seen to work basically through the everyday details of life, then pastors' attentiveness to mundane administrative tasks is sharing directly in God's work in the church. Unless a pastor needs constant involvement in high-level policy decisions in order to feel confident, we clergy can reflect on the significance of our routine administrative tasks and affirm ourselves. The ordinary is, indeed, extraordinary.

Affirming our administrative faithfulness is a healthy step toward conserving our own self-cohesion. We have observed throughout how injuries to pastors' self-esteem are a far more serious harm than previously thought. Injuries to self-esteem, whether received or self-inflicted, tend to trigger either aggressive responses or a collapse of confidence that reverberates throughout everything else injured pastors do. Affirmations, in contrast, are a far more serious good than previously thought. Received affirmations and self-affirmations strengthen pastors' values, and nurture their capacity to be empathic with others and with their own selves. Affirmations fortify pastors against threats to their self-cohesion and heal injuries already sustained.

Affirming our administrative contribution helps us reach a cohesive state where we can say "yes" to the apostle Paul's pronouncement that honor attends a person when that person is willing to contribute to God's church whatever he or she is able. All gifts of self and time are needed, and none is more valuable than any other. Affirming our administrative work can also help usher us back to why we entered church work in the first place—to gather as children around Jesus, and to do our part as part of that loving crowd.

Cohesive pastors who endure and affirm the rigors of routine administration are equipped to use time competently. For example, they can use time in ways that do not necessarily contribute to the subjective satisfaction of the congregation or to their own selves, that is, to feelings of being pain-free and happy. Pastors endure discomfort at times because they realize that subjective satisfaction itself is not a sufficient criterion of goodness. "We could take a vote right now and it would seem to solve the problem," said a pastor to a turbulent church council, "but that would just sweep it under the table. We need time to live with this problem, to face what it means for us personally and as a congregation. That will cause us all some pain, but we will be better for it in the long run." Cohesive pastors establish lead times, discovery times, reaction times, and recovery times that may not bring immediate soothing to parishioners, but which pastors know are vital for healing and wholeness.

Cohesive administrators tend also to be practical guardians of time. They realize that time is the central structuring resource in ministry in that it controls the use of all other resources: pastors' abilities, talents, training, experience, and motivations. They approach time in pragmatic ways that allow others and themselves to be effective in loving, leading, teaching, or consoling.

AFFIRMING OTHERS

The Chicago School of Economics is famous for espousing the position that individuals make choices and decisions in a rational manner, and that given the freedom to do so, individuals acting in their own best interests will come up with the most efficient means possible for meeting goals and handling problems. This is called the principle of rational optimizing behavior.

Can we pastors affirm that laity act with optimal responsiveness in church administration? We know contrary behavior too well—in others and in ourselves. Like the apostle Paul we know that all of us do the things we would not do, and do not do the things that we would.

A businessman in church once said, "If you put a group of bright business people together and gave them the same facts, they'll come up with roughly the same answer. This seems not to be true about churches, however." Why the trailing comment? What did he see in the administrative work in the church? With a similar reflection Martin Luther King, Jr. once lamented, "More and more I feel that people of ill will have used time much more effectively than people of good will."[4]

And yet we clergy must hope. We must hope that laity in administration can be optimally effective, and that they can be, and are, means for God's work in the world. More than that, we must live "as if" that is true, responding to laity in the most affirming ways, even while realizing their limitations.

Walter Brueggemann points to the basic reason for affirming laity in administration: "What God does first and best and most is to trust his people with their moments in history. He trusts them to do what must be done for the sake of his whole community."[5] Parishioners often violate that trust, but God nevertheless not only gives them responsibility for the congregation but also trusts that they will do a decent job.

Reverend Marten's seminary professor was half right. He was right in suggesting that the preferences of "the untutored many" should be foremost, for God has entrusted his people with the community's moment in history. He was off base, however, in calling laity "untutored." Not only are church leaders sophisticated in ways of organization, but pastors can also trust that God continues to tutor laity all along the way. Church administration is not just a partnership between pastor and laity, but also between God and the people.

Clergy can, and should, affirm laity by affirming trust in them. Trusting laity in administration is an intentional act, not just an automatic assumption. It is an acknowledgment of laity's integrity, and an expression of clergy's willingness to join them and be influenced by them.

Affirming laity in church administration helps preserve pastors' self-cohesion. Trusting others instills within pastors a reassurance that their environment is honest and caring. Simultaneously, trusting others also inclines pastors to be trustworthy themselves, and thus reinforces pride in their moral character. We not only trust others in the manner in which we trust ourselves, we also come to trust ourselves in the manner we trust others. Trusting laity and acting trustworthy solidifies clergy's self-cohesion.

Affirming laity by affirming trust in them also guides pastors in their use of time. For example, except in emergency situations, affirming pastors do not spend administrative time trying to wrestle control from laity. Instead, they use time to promote partnership in leading the church. In the same spirit Reverend Marten initially brought to the council, they see their main administrative task as bringing people closer together and closer to God, trusting that people will then respond with cooperative and caring hearts. "Let us spend the first part of our council time with Scripture and prayer, and then catch up on how everyone is doing. Our ministry to others begins with ministry to one another, and with a reminder that we are children of God trying to love as we have been loved."

Cohesive pastors lead toward fullness of time. Their administrative efforts reverberate with the spiritual mandate of their calling:

> "The Spirit of the Lord is upon
> me,
> because he has anointed me
> to bring good news to the
> poor.
> He has sent me to proclaim
> release to the captives

and recovery of sight to the
blind,
to let the oppressed go free,
to proclaim the year of the
Lord's favor."
(Luke 4:18-19)

Chapter Six

Self/Time Management
in Personal Maintenance

Reverend James turned the car around. He had been heading back to church, but something inside prompted him to alter his course. He knew he was doing the right thing. He wasn't sure how he knew, it just felt right, as something natural in his bones. A slight smile appeared on his face as he stepped on the accelerator and headed for home.

Self-Cohesion and Personal Maintenance

Throughout these pages another area of pastors' work has been alluded to besides pastoral care, preaching, and church administration. That area is personal maintenance. We clergy must minister to our personal self. We rightly make our personal self an object of care. That is not narcissism. It is regard for our self that honors God's love for us. It is regard for our self that leads us to honor others.

Personal maintenance is a basically natural inclination within us. Each of us, for example, has an innate tendency to care for our body, to preserve our integrity, and to nurture our relationships. Knowledge of how to do this is partly intuitive and partly learned over our lifetime. Each of us also possesses a self-righting mechanism that tells us when we are out of balance and need to realign for our own good health.

Personal maintenance of our body, integrity, and relationships is central for preserving firm self-cohesion. We experience a state of well-being (firm self-cohesion) when we are at home with our body, at home with our conscience, and at home with others. Reverend James's impulse to turn around may not have come from duty's obligation but from his heart's desire to find home again.

Personal maintenance, however, may be devalued or avoided. On the one hand, personal maintenance itself can threaten us. Caring for our body typically forces us to confront signs of our aging, and to face disturbing visions of our own funeral. Attending to our integrity may make us realize that we are often wrong, and that we are no more special than anyone else. Looking after our relationships may lift up memories of having been deeply hurt by others we counted on, and of lost opportunities to love and be loved.

As a result of these discomforting experiences, we may ignore our body, resist looking inward, or deal with people on a superficial level. We clergy must wisely recognize how threats to our self-cohesion arising from our efforts to maintain our self-cohesion may suppress those very efforts.

On the other hand, religious orientations, cultural expectations, or family teachings may undermine personal maintenance efforts. For example, theological teachings that degrade the body will curtail a wide range of ways to personally maintain the fullness of our bodily life. As a result, our self-cohesion is weakened. We clergy must wisely recognize those external deterrents to the personal maintenance of our body, integrity, and relationships.

Weakened self-cohesion as a result of inadequate personal maintenance impairs our capacities for living and using time fully. For example, we may minimize "play time" needed for refreshing our body and soul. We may avoid "slow time" needed for prolonged emotional honesty with ourself. We may relinquish "protected time" needed for the preserving of our relationships.

How we manage our self and time in the process of personal maintenance also affects how we minister to the life-time of parishioners. Once again, not only is our own cohesion at stake, but also the cohesion of those whose lives we touch.

Our efforts to respond wisely can share the psalmist's prayerful request: "So teach us to count our days that we may gain a wise heart" (Ps. 90:12). God's limit-setting on our time can help us take life seriously. Reflecting on the stretch of our lived time connects to our conduct, to the ways we try to live our time most fully. Personal maintenance of body, integrity, and relationships is wisely carried out not so much in the shadow of the fear of death, as in the light of God's intentions for our limited days.

Our affirmation of ourself and others in personal maintenance is sustained by the belief that God is constantly creating a new and right spirit within us. No one is a lost cause, because God is continually re-creating all of us. Everyone is a conception of the Creator who will finish his handiwork in his own good time.

BEING WISE ABOUT OURSELF

"This is my body." Jesus' words at the Last Supper about his body are more than symbolic. They witness to the centrality of the body in our personal existence. That Jesus gave up his body to be broken for us meant not that the body was evil or an encumbrance that must be shed. Instead Jesus is proclaiming that he offers up *himself* through that which is created and intimately one with his very spirit—his body. Jesus' sacrifice of his body, furthermore, was more than a "sign" of his inner self's love for God and humanity. To sacrifice his body meant to offer up *his very self*. It was the ultimate commitment of his embodied self that opened redemptive possibilities for us all.

Jesus knew that we live and move and have our being through our body. He reflected the spirit of the Hebrews, who in the Old Testament show a remarkable sense of the unity of the human being. Nowhere in the Old Testament is a person described as simply a soul inhabiting a body, and the body is never depicted simply as a casing for the soul. We are not all body, but all that we are we are through our body. The restoration and personal maintenance of the self is always bodily, for that is how we are in the world, as body-selves.

Self-cohesion stays firm when we live through our body fully. That means letting our bodily feelings come strong and forceful: letting our nerve endings tingle when listening to inspiring music, letting our heart ache for those who suffer, letting our whole body absorb the pleasure of a hug or the sexual stimulation of our partner's body. It means running our fingers through the soil and knowing we are part of it, breathing in the winds of spring and winter, feeling in rhythm with the seasons and with the ebb and flow of life. It means savoring our vigor as well as the decline that comes with aging. It means sensing our own death and greeting it from afar.

Living through our body means using our body to know how others are experiencing life, and to know how it feels

to walk in their body-self with its dimensions, skills, limitations, and looks. It means trusting our body to tell us
what is right and wrong before our head does, and trusting
our implicit bodily reactions to what people say and do. It
means embracing the body as a channel by which the
Spirit warms us and prompts us into action, and as the
means by which we know that Christ is with us. Wise
personal maintenance involves fostering a life lived
through the fullness of our meaning-giving body.

Failure to maintain our body-self weakens our self-
cohesion. Some pastors respond to the body as an object
to be controlled. "I don't give my body a vote," said one
"type A" pastor. The body was considered an encumbrance that kept the pastor from succeeding. Signals from
the pastor's body alerting him to the need for rest and
balance—tension, chest pains, sleeplessness—were tran-
quilized by exercise and medication. Constantly "plugged
in," he accomplished much but at the expense of health
and relationships.

Other clergy withdraw from their body. One pastor cut
herself off from most body sensations because of a previous bout with cancer. She was reluctant to feel through
her body, let alone pay much attention to it, for to do so
caused great anxiety. "When I focus on my body I sense
the horizon at the far end of life, and it scares me." As a
result of withdrawing from her body, the range of her
emotional reactions was narrow. She could not truly re-
joice, or feel deep sadness, either for herself or others. She
had difficulty opening the minutes and investing them
with meaning.

Other pastors alienate themselves from their body. One
pastor who yearned to live "a Christian life" demeaned the
body as a source of sin. He strove to free himself not only

from bodily impulses, but also from the full weight of being a physical self.

Unfortunately he then failed to achieve his goal. Rather than living the Christian life more fully, he lived it less fully. His body, for example, was no longer a means for feeling into the moral situations of people, for sensing within himself the moral meanings and struggles of others. Without bodily feelings guiding his moral understanding, he was reduced to disembodied reason. Guidelines for ethical living were pronounced from the pulpit in an arid, compassion-diminished manner. Alienated from his body as a means for moral perception, he became alienated from empathic connectedness with others.[1]

Although we might not regard our body in exactly these ways, they demonstrate our tendencies to divest the body of importance, or to abstract ourselves from bodily concreteness, or to actually estrange ourselves from our body. Ignorance, uncertainty, and shame about our physical self create disturbances in our self and distance in our relationships—the loss of healthy self-cohesion.

There are times when minimizing the body is appropriate. When panic floods our body, we need to "use our head" rather than "go with our feelings." Before submitting to medical tests or surgery, we may try to momentarily distance ourself from our body in order to maintain our composure. Those who are being physically or sexually abused may need to feel disembodied in order to survive. Those martyred for the faith may likewise minimize their physical self: "The body they may kill. God's truth abideth still." Typically, however, we clergy weaken our self-cohesion when we fail to live fully through our body.

Weakened self-cohesion due to failures to live in the thickness of our body results in failures to live in the thickness of our time. When naturally integrated, our body places us in the sweep of time. It unites us directly to the world, and to the vitality of the present moment—the primary tense of life. Our body, anchoring us in the present, gives us an assurance of life's substance and our reality. Simultaneously, our body gives us a felt sense of the past and of who we have been, and allows us a felt sense of the future and of who we can become.

An integrated body, furthermore, creates an integrated sense of the past, present, and future flowing into one another. When we live in the body fully, we do not dichotomize time, or try to repress the ambiguity of temporal modes overlapping and influencing one another. We experience bodily that we are simultaneously all we have been, currently are, and possibly can be.

When our body is poorly integrated and our self-cohesion weakened, the present moment may seem vague or empty. It may seem undependable if not unreal. Without the density of bodily feelings our sense of living fully in the present is diminished. Similarly, when the body is repressed, the past is remembered as dry memory rather than re-experienced through the body's felt sense of events and relationships. The future, likewise, becomes untouchable. We lose the capacity to imagine, through our feelings and sensations, new possibilities for our self.

Pastors alienated from their body have difficulty as well with the integration and ambiguity of time, where past, present, and future comingle. Time, instead, becomes dissociated. The present is made a time box separated from the past and the future as time boxes. Present action tends to die in the present, without the pastor having any sense of the action's future consequences. The past is made past, without the pastor understanding the past and rendering it useful. The future is a vague unknown without the power to beckon the pastor to new possibilities, and without the potential for restructuring what has been. Without a firm body-self, the temporal world around us is vapid, if not meaningless.

Body estrangement and weakened self-cohesion also lead to ineffective use of time. When normally integrated, our body participates in our decisions. Within our body we have implicit, felt understandings about situations and relationships. Our body vibrates with impressions about people. Our body perceives meanings in circumstances before our mind does. We habitually "trust our feelings" about things. In our thinking we make these implicit bodily feelings explicit, and carry them forward by reflection and evaluation. Our implicit bodily knowing becomes the basis of our thought-out decisions.

Ignoring or demeaning our bodily feelings about situations undercuts effective time management. For example, without listening to our body register "too much," we may languish in prolonged beginnings, where we are always "getting ready" but never proceeding. We miss the clues our body typically gives for when to act. Similarly, without consulting our felt sense of the right time, we may initiate premature closures, where we do not give enough time for a new program to develop. Then again, we may delay closure on projects that our deeper bodily awareness suggests should have been terminated earlier. Time management relies upon incarnational wisdom.

Diminished cohesion resulting from divestment in our body also affects our lived time with parishioners. Those of us unable to fully embrace our body have difficulty devoting time to traumas of parishioners, such as sexual or physical abuse, handicaps, and fragility that reflect an unbearable assault on our bodily existence. Uneasy with our body, we also tend to spend less time with those who are dying, and with whose who grieve. Their pain, and the fright that death often elicits, leads us to limit time with them.

Finally, when cut off from the fullness of bodily life, we fail to develop a mature and sensitive spirituality. In the fullness of embodiment we sense that the force that drives the tree to grow drives our heart to beat. Through our body we know that we pulsate with the rhythms of nature, of seedtime and harvest, of day and night, of birth and death. Through our body we sense a mystical participation in all cosmic events, with which we are inwardly as well as outwardly interwoven.

I remember sitting on my back porch one June afternoon hoping the dark clouds would not pass by. "Come on. Come on," I cried out loud to them. "We need the rain." Still looking upward I began to chant in imitation of an Indian rain dance: "Ha ya ya ya, ha ya ya ya, ha ya ya ya," copying what I'd heard in some western movie as a kid. I then began to move my feet to the chant: Stomp stomp stomp stomp, stomp stomp stomp stomp, playfully inviting the cloud spirits to come and stay.

Strangely enough as I did this, I began to feel my body connected to those clouds, as though my rhythmic movements and repetitive sounds were part of the cosmos, vibrating with creation's vibrations and taken seriously. I felt light, airy, peaceful. The Hopi Indians say there is no difference between dancing and praying, and I guess I was praying then, throwing my body into the world, embracing it, merging with it, as if the molecules of me and the molecules of the trees and earth were one. And they are. Beyond traditional form, I was praying to God, whose creation is the primary scripture, and my body in it the primary place of divine-human communion.

Without living our body fully, we miss an awareness of liturgical time: God's tranquil, unhurried meter of time in life, the regular rhythms of God's creative energy set within us, our body as the sacred vessel by which God reveals the interrelationship of all with all at every moment, and the fullness of time when God meets us with Word made flesh. Our capacity to reveal time to parishioners is diminished when we fail to personally maintain the fullness of our body-self.

BEING WISE ABOUT OTHERS

When the self-cohesion of pastors is weakened, their capacity for acting with integrity is weakened. The more severe their fragmentation, the more difficulty they have with truthfulness, sincerity, authenticity, and commitment—those virtues associated with integrity. In one classic case, a pastor who felt crushed by the actions of his consistory left the hot water running all night in the parsonage in order to drive up the church's utility bill. He was not basically an immoral man; just one whose present state of collapsed self-cohesion incapacitated his strength to maintain integrity.

Fragmented clergy, however, must be encouraged to guard their integrity and to act with integrity, no matter how angry or inclined to withdraw they may feel. Maintaining their integrity is a key way to preserve what remnant of self-cohesion they still possess, and to build toward restoration of their self-cohesion. Self-cohesion itself is strengthened when our integrity is personally maintained. Integrity is a necessity for wholeness of self. It is essential for being truly human, for being an individual who seeks not simply length of days, but quality of days.

Integrity is an action more than a state of the pastor's self. It involves self-reflection, assessment of moral decisions, confession, and efforts to change. Integrity is the action of trying to maintain a morally sensitive way of life. Our self-cohesion stays firm when in spite of failings and shortcomings we experience ourselves still striving for moral clarity and a life of valor.

Efforts to maintain integrity can threaten our self-cohesion, however. One pastor took a book I had written and held it out away from him saying, "I tend not to like to look too closely at myself." He was being more than humorous, and was representing more than just his own avoidance. For a variety of reasons it is difficult for us clergy to seriously confront ourselves.

Our focus in this section, however, is on how *parishioners* may impede clergy's efforts at personal maintenance of integrity. Clergy must be wise to these ways lest they abandon their integrity efforts and thus weaken their self-cohesion.

Parishioners may inadvertently contribute to pastors' disregard for their own integrity. For example, they may dissuade clergy from self-scrutiny by their well-meaning praise. C. Welton Gaddy tells in his confessional book *A Soul Under Siege: Surviving Clergy Depression,* how he succumbed to "the siren songs of mythology" offered up by his parishioners: "You are just incredible, totally unreal"; "You can do anything you set out to do"; "You are so strong and confident"; "You work so hard and do so much good"; "You have such a remarkable faith." These spoken attitudes were not so much unrealistic expectations that caused him grief as they were idealistic affirmations that enticed him into avoiding honesty with himself. He urges us when hearing such statements to have "the wisdom to allow a smile to cross [our] face, and the honesty quickly to say to [ourselves], Don't you believe it. Don't you believe it for even one second."[2]

Parishioners may defensively contribute to clergy's avoidance of integrity maintenance. Parishioners carry normal to unrealistic expectations for pastors that they do not want pastors to thwart. Consequently, they typically do not want to hear about pastors' integrity problems unless they are minor or humorous. When one preacher spoke of his often unsuccessful struggles to live by the truths in the biblical text for the day, a member let him know she did not want to hear of his difficulties with discipleship. Out of nonsupport and fears of rejection, we clergy may hide our own true feelings and thus perpetuate avoidance of moral introspection.

Parishioners may coercively contribute to the erosion of clergy's integrity. Very often parishioners ask for special favors that require the pastor to compromise his or her standards. A parishioner's plea of "just this once" is usually "for my advantage" or "for my comfort." Parishioners are also notorious for using money, status, and politics to pressure pastors into compliance with their wishes. When pastors say no, or are not able to make adjustments satisfying to the requesters, the latter react with shades of anger or withdrawal. "Being true to yourself is the best policy but it doesn't make everyone happy," observed one pastor.

Under these implicit or explicit threats, pastors often compromise their values. Unable to live with the resulting moral dissonance in their lives, when they have done something that cannot be squared with their values, they tend either to construct rationalizations for their behavior, or to try to cover the pain of their self-betrayal. In either case the renewing process of integrity maintenance is evaded.

Finally, some parishioners may assaultively undercut clergy's integrity efforts. For example, parishioners may accuse the pastor of greed or self-centeredness. They may categorize him or her as morally weak or lacking integrity. Concerted efforts to get the pastor fired may result in public exposure of the pastor's supposed sins.

When the context is threatening, pastors typically defend themselves against the charges, as well as strive to protect their self-esteem. Using the comments from parishioners for moral introspection does not usually happen when clergy feel in an unsafe environment. Onslaughts discourage soul-searching. As a result, pastors' defensive self-justifications displace those self-assessments necessary for the healthy maintenance of their integrity.

When clergy's self-cohesion is weakened by inability to maintain integrity, their capacity for using time adequately suffers. For example, integrity requires "slow-time." Self-introspection and moral discernment are complex, often painful processes needing unhurried, sustained immersion in feeling and thought. Integrity-fragmented clergy have difficulty staying in slow-time. Instead they tend to respond in ways that foreshorten time for reflection. They may function as mechanic moralists, working with set procedures that they deem should be followed in every moral situation, or they may function as dogmatic moralists, applying legalistic rules to even the most complex situations.

Less rationally rigid approaches may also eschew slow-time necessary for fairness to persons and their lived-time.

Pastors may function as intuitive moralists, acting on instinct and a sudden sense of what is right, or as prophetic moralists, issuing indictments against particular evils without reference to guiding principles, and without devising effective responses. Slow-time tends to be deserted by clergy with weakened integrity.

Integrity-fragmented clergy may also respond in "time-bites." When cohesion is firm, clergy react as if their integrity is connected to the whole of their lived-time. They sense, as well, that the integrity of a parishioner, and the values and principles that integrity secures, shape the pattern of that parishioner's entire life. "One's life as a whole—conceived temporally as having a beginning, middle, and end—is the principle subject of integrity as it applies to persons," says ethicist Martin Benjamin.[3] Benjamin should have added a modifier: "for those who enjoy firm integrity."

When cohesion is weak, clergy are less inclined to connect integrity with the whole sweep of lived-time. They think and evaluate in "time-bites," in small sequences of time, rather than try to comprehend the longer history of themselves or others. For example, they take a moment as a measure or reflection of the whole lifetime of a parishioner. They make that moment in the parishioner's life the center of an interpretation about who that parishioner is and about his or her worth. Unfortunately that moment is usually a moment of weakness, which becomes the time-bite tag the parishioner is stuck with.

Time-bite thinking also manifests itself when clergy take their own moment of behavior as a validation of their whole self. For example, some clergy perform a specific act of charity and thus surmise that they are good. Or they may confess an indiscretion and conclude that they are truthful. Or they may commit an offense and interpret that their whole life has been a waste. Broad-time thinking that honors the course of a person's life is minimized when integrity is not maintained.

Time in ministry does not make one mature. Integrity in one's time in ministry makes one mature. Wise pastors steadfastly maintain their integrity, and thus their cohesion and effective use of time.

AFFIRMING OURSELF AND OTHERS

The state of our self-cohesion also affects how we relate to others. When pastors are riddled with self-doubt, for instance, their capacity for responding with empathy to the joys or sorrows of others is diminished. Cohesion shapes relationships.

But firm relationships, just like integrity, are also key means by which self-cohesion is preserved and restored. When a wounded pastor feels a tender, understanding hand placed on his shoulder, healing begins. When a lonely pastor is warmly invited to join a circle of others, her pain subsides. Personal maintenance of our relationships is essential for firm self-cohesion.

Tending our relationships invites hurt. One pastor said, "Relationships always leave you with a limp. You always get injured sooner or later." The inevitability of pain in relationships can prompt us to disconnect. "It's better to try to feel self-contained and not needful of others than it is to want to be included and be left out," lamented one pastor. In spite of all the talk in churches about the importance of relationships, pastors as a group tend to feel isolated and to foster being isolated. Such a condition both expresses lost self-cohesion as well as contributes to it.

We clergy need to maintain our relationships no matter how painful they may be at times. One way we can persist in this is through the power of affirmation. What we can affirm about ourselves and others is that each one of us strives to feel a human heart beating next to our own. Although our efforts may be misguided or excessive, each of us in our own way reaches for the hand of another. Our lived-time is the story of attempts to overcome strangeness and find space for intimacy. Personal maintenance of our relationships can be sustained by the vision of each person poised to extend and receive understanding. In the presence of such yearnings we are already connected even before we know one another.

When our relationships are firm, our uses of time are beneficial. For example, we uphold the necessity for both quality and quantity of time in our relationships. We do not succumb to the false dichotomy raised in the question, "Is it the amount of time set aside for others that is most important or is it making the moments count?" Length of time spent must have quality to it before it becomes a blessing. Quality of time only develops when sufficient time is spent. Most often the false dichotomy question is raised when a person's relationships are ambiguous or stressful.

When relationships are firm, we also tend to focus our time. For example, rather than devote bits of time to a multitude of relationships, we are able to enjoy in depth those special relationships that genuinely suit us. Similarly, instead of trying to be "all things to all people," we focus time on being the best person we can be with those lives that more immediately touch ours. Without guilt, we are also able to focus time on individuals whose needs are not only real, but also solvable. All people are children of God, but some manifest problems for which no amount of time can alleviate. Focused time in ministry tries to make the best use of the resources given us.

Affirming relationships also encourages us to humanize time. We are moved to help others make sense of their life-time journey, to make it bearable. We may urge others to reminisce so that meanings central to their life will continue to sustain them. Looking back over our years, we can all benefit from reaffirming those beliefs and purposes that have guided our daily existence. We can hold them up as cherished values we carry, and which carry us, to a peaceful end.

We may assist others in previewing their life-time. A pastor may envision and articulate the contours of a young parishioner's development. Then again, the pastor may be a supportive, encouraging partner while an older parishioner rehearses new roles. With images of hope, we clergy can preview the fulfillment of Christ's promises for eternal life. Previewing helps self-formation, and the future state of our self-cohesion.

Finally, we humanize time by awakening others to the power of their present, the primary tense of life. A great phrase booms consistently out of the Scriptures: "*Now* is the time." Now, the present moment, is infinitely significant because every moment is the now of a decision. Now, the present moment, is a religious event, for it radiates with the purposes of God. The present time is not meaningless. It is the occasion for living the fullness of time, and in doing that to experience something of eternity. We clergy enhance the lived-time of ourselves and others by evoking the awesomeness of the now.

Notes

Introduction: Life Time

1. These issues are discussed more fully in: Robert L. Randall, *Pastor and Parish: The Psychological Core of Ecclesiastical Conflicts* (New York: Human Sciences Press, 1988).

2. Robert L. Randall, *What People Expect From Church: Why Meeting the Needs of People Is More Important than Church Meetings* (Nashville: Abingdon Press, 1992).

3. Self/Time Management in Pastoral Care

1. *Selfobject* is a term and concept developed by the late Heinz Kohut. It is the basis of his new orientation toward psychotherapy called "Self Psychology" (see bibliography). A cogent discussion of selfobject can be found in: Robert L. Randall, *The Eternal Triangle: Pastor, Spouse, & Congregation* (Minneapolis: Fortress Press, 1992).

2. Reported by Dr. Arch Hart of Fuller who conducted the research.

4. Self/Time Management in Preaching

1. Walter J. Burghardt, *Preaching: The Art and the Craft* (New York: Paulist Press, 1987), p. 190.

5. Self/Time Management in Church Administration

1. William H. Leach, *Church Administration: A Survey of Modern Executive Methods* (New York: George H. Doran Company, 1926), pp. 13-14.

2. Franz Kafka, "The Metamorphosis," in *The Penal Colony*, trans. Willa and Edwin Muir (New York: Schocken Books, 1948).

3. Robert E. Kelley, *The Power of Followership: How to Create Leaders People Want to Follow and Followers Who Lead Themselves* (New York: Doubleday Currency, 1992), p. 7.

4. Martin Luther King, Jr., *Why We Can't Wait* (New York: 1964), p. 86.

5. Walter Brueggemann, "The Trusted Creature," *Catholic Biblical Quarterly*, 31 (1969): 488.

6. Self/Time Management in Personal Maintenance

1. See James B. Nelson, "The Moral Context of Counseling," in *The Pastor as Counselor*, ed. Earl E. Shelp and Ronald H. Sunderland (New York: The Pilgrim Press, 1991), pp. 54-75.

2. C. Welton Gaddy, *A Soul Under Siege: Surviving Clergy Depression* (Louisville: Westminster/John Knox Press, 1991), p. 38.

3. Martin Benjamin, *Splitting the Difference: Compromise and Integrity in Ethics and Politics* (Lawrence: University of Kansas, 1990), p. 59.

Selected Bibliography

Benjamin, Martin. *Splitting the Difference: Compromise and Integrity in Ethics and Politics.* Lawrence: University of Kansas, 1990.

Brueggemann, Walter. "The Trusted Creature." *Catholic Biblical Quarterly* 31 (1969).

Burghardt, Walter J. *Preaching: The Art and the Craft.* New York: Paulist Press, 1987.

Covey, Stephen R. *The Seven Habits of Highly Effective People: Restoring the Character Ethic.* New York: Simon & Schuster, 1989.

Eyre, Richard and Linda. *Lifebalance.* New York: Ballantine Books, 1987.

Gaddy, C. Welton. *A Soul Under Siege: Surviving Clergy Depression.* Louisville: Westminster/John Knox Press, 1991.

Hall, Edward T. *The Dance of Life: The Other Dimension of Time.* New York: Anchor Press/Doubleday, 1983.

Kafka, Franz. "The Metamorphosis." *The Penal Colony.* Trans. Willa and Edwin Muir. New York: Schocken Books, 1948.

Kelley, Robert E. *The Power of Followership: How to Create Leaders People Want to Follow and Followers Who Lead Themselves.* New York: Doubleday Currency, 1992.

King, Martin Luther, Jr. *Why We Can't Wait.* New York, 1964.

Kohut, Heinz. *The Restoration of the Self.* New York: International Universities Press, 1977.

Lasher, Margot. *The Art and Practice of Compassion and Empathy.* New York: Jeremy P. Tarcher/Perigee, 1992.

Leach, William H. *Church Administration: A Survey of Modern Executive Methods.* New York: George H. Doran Company, 1926.

Lindgren, Alvin J. *Foundations for Purposeful Church Administration.* New York: Abingdon Press, 1965.

McCabe, Joseph E. *Better Preaching and Better Pastoring.* Philadelphia: The Westminster Press, 1973.

Nelson, James B. "The Moral Context of Counseling." *The Pastor as Counselor.* Ed. Earl E. Shelp and Ronald H. Sunderland. New York: The Pilgrim Press, 1991.

Randall, Robert L. *Pastor and Parish: The Psychological Core of Ecclesiastical Conflicts.* New York: Human Sciences Press, 1988.

____. *The Eternal Triangle: Pastor, Spouse, & Congregation.* Minneapolis: Fortress Press, 1992.

____. *What People Expect from Church: Why Meeting the Needs of People Is More Important than Church Meetings.* Nashville: Abingdon Press, 1992.

Servan-Schreiber, Jean Louis. *The Art of Time.* Trans. Franklin Philip. Reading, Mass.: Addison-Wesley Publishing Company, 1988.

Thomas, James M. *Individual Integrity.* Savannah, Ga: Castlemarsh Publications, 1984.

Tidwell, Charles A. *Church Administration: Effective Leadership for Ministry.* Nashville: Broadman Press, 1985.